FINDING
JOY
in the
MIDST
of
SORROW

ONE FAMILY'S JOURNEY FROM TRAGEDY
TO TRIUMPH...AND PURPOSE

Mike McCrum

with Debbie McCrum

WESTBOW
P R E S S®
A DIVISION OF THOMAS NELSON
& ZONDERVAN

WestBow Press books may be ordered through booksellers or by contacting:

WestBow Press
A Division of Thomas Nelson & Zondervan
1663 Liberty Drive
Bloomington, IN 47403
www.westbowpress.com
1 (866) 928-1240

ISBN: 978-1-5127-5825-2 (sc)
ISBN: 978-1-5127-5826-9 (hc)
ISBN: 978-1-5127-5824-5 (e)

Library of Congress Control Number: 2016916199

Print information available on the last page.

WestBow Press rev. date: 11/23/2016

CONTENTS

Before Words... xi
The Story Within the Story........................... xvii

Chapter 1   First Faith 1
Chapter 2   The Accident.................................. 8
Chapter 3   Sawmill Revival 15
Chapter 4   Cinderella.................................... 22
Chapter 5   5:55 P.M. 28
Chapter 6   Jungle Bound................................ 36
Chapter 7   Bloodshed 43
Chapter 8   Left Behind 50
Chapter 9   Blind Man 66
Chapter 10 No Mistake 73
Chapter 11 Mission:937 84
Chapter 12 Identity Crisis.............................. 92
Chapter 13 Forgiven 99
Chapter 14 Family Secrets............................ 107
Chapter 15 The Launch 117
Chapter 16 Unwanted Detour 122
Chapter 17 A Promise Kept........................... 130
Chapter 18 The Perfect Storm....................... 139
Chapter 19 Pit of Despair 158
Chapter 20 Reluctant Professor...................... 165

Chapter 21 The Toilet Aisle 172
Chapter 22 Unshackled 179
Chapter 23 Snowmageddon 185
Chapter 24 The Great Sadness 191
Chapter 25 Waves of Mercy............................ 197
Chapter 26 Why?... 204
Chapter 27 Our Father 212
Chapter 28 There's More............................... 220
Chapter 29 Surprise! 226

After Words... 235
Great is Thy Faithfulness............................... 239
Developing a Family Purpose 241
Acknowledgements... 243
Notes 245

For our children,

Destiny
Cherith
Amber
Robby

and grandchildren,

Will
Madelynn
Abigail
Aiden
Lily
Ansley

and the generations to come...

and for those on the outside looking in.

We will tell the next generation
the praiseworthy deeds of the Lord...
and they in turn would tell their children.
Then they would put their trust in God.

Psalm 78:4-7 (NIV)

BEFORE WORDS

On May 5, 2014 tragedy struck our family. What happened on that day would change our lives... forever.

I was driving to the Atlanta International Airport to pick up our thirty-three year-old daughter, Cherith. She was returning from a company cruise of the Mediterranean. It was the trip of a lifetime.

In the last entry of her diary Cherith had written, "This was the best day of my life!" Now, she was on the last leg of her flight home from Rome with a two-hour layover in New York's JFK airport. We could hardly wait to see her!

It was 8:00 p.m. when my wife, Debbie, called and said to turn around and come back home. Cherith had phoned to say she had attempted to board the Delta aircraft, but got off when she suddenly became ill. Her plans were to spend the night in a nearby hotel and catch a standby flight home in the morning.

There was something not quite right with how Cherith had ended their conversation. She said, "Mom, would you pray for me?"

Fortunately, Theresa Blakey, her coworker and traveling buddy, insisted on staying behind with her. She called an hour later on Cherith's cell phone. "Mrs. McCrum. Cherith has become unconscious. The EMTs have arrived. We're on our way to the hospital."

What was going on?

By the tone in Theresa's voice the situation seemed rather serious. But, surely Cherith would be okay. Maybe this quick trip to the Jamaica Medical Center was only precautionary.

Debbie and I were hit broadside with confusion. Having to interpret a family crisis hundreds of miles away through a brief cell phone conversation made the situation difficult to process.

At midnight the emergency room doctor called to give an update. Cherith was still unconscious and they were working hard to find the problem. At the same time our other two daughters Destiny and Amber, both nurses themselves, were on the phone with ER personnel, trying to get answers.

That's when reality sank in—Cherith was fighting for her life.

We were struck with unwanted pangs of anxiety and fear. This just couldn't be happening. One day our daughter is fine and healthy; the next day she's on life support. What reason did we have to hold out hope?

At 3:00 a.m. the phone rang. It was the ER doctor. The voice on the other end was somber and to the point. "Mr. McCrum we have found the problem—a large mass on your daughter's brain stem. However, the tumor is inoperable."

There was an eerie pause. My emotions started caving in around me. Then came the words I didn't want to hear. "We've done all we can do."

***

In the weeks that followed, concerned friends would come up to Debbie and me and ask, "How are you guys dealing with all this?"

Even in the pain both of us had good reasons to go on living, to thrive, not just survive. God had been faithful to us time and again. Could we not trust him in our weakest hour?

We held on tightly to the words Jeremiah wrote as he watched Jerusalem, Daughter of Zion, being overtaken by the Babylonian army. Despite their tragedy, the weeping prophet provided this hope:

> The steadfast love of the LORD never ceases; his mercies never come to an end; they are new every morning; great is your faithfulness.
> (Lamentations 3:22-23)

Every day it seemed God's mercies were unfolding before our eyes. I began to openly share all the surprising things God was doing. The feedback was unanimous: "Mike, you've got to write all this down. We need to know how to go through life's tragedies."

We received further encouragement from Dr. Crawford Loritts, Senior Pastor at Fellowship Bible Church in Roswell, Georgia where I work and Debbie and I worship. One day he stopped me in the staff hallway to say, "Mike, I believe there is a story inside you waiting to be written."

What was God saying? He wanted us to document his faithfulness to our family and leave a written legacy for the generations to come.

Passing down a family purpose to our children has always been an important theme in the Bible. God's purpose for Israel was declared in Deuteronomy 6:4-9. Families were to love him wholeheartedly. Parents would write the *Shema* (Hebrew prayer of faith) on the doorposts of their house and teach it diligently to their children as a constant reminder for them to walk in God's ways.

Our family purpose is taken from Psalm 78:4-7. These verses of Scripture are framed on our dining room wall between photos of our parents. It is an impactful reminder that our marriage exists "to tell the next generation about the mighty deeds of God so that they can put their trust in him."

Finding Joy in the Midst of Sorrow is written for our grandkids and their children. Like a treasure map, it is intended to help navigate them through the journey of life. We've provided reliable clues and valuable secrets to guide them to their buried treasure—heaven.

In addition, Dr. Loritts has challenged us to "leave spiritual footprints in the sands of time for future generations."[1] It is Poppy and Grammy's desire to leave clear, easy to see, deep tracks for our grandchildren to follow—footprints that will help them rely on God's enduring faithfulness.

Finding Joy in the Midst of Sorrow is also a story God wanted told to encourage other families. Its pages are meant to inspire those just starting out on their adventure, to give hope to those who are stuck in sorrow along the way, and to bring joy and peace to those nearing the finish line.

There is no doubt God has ordained a path for you and your family to take. Most likely it will involve risks that stretch you to the limit. But God promises it is one that brings purpose, freedom, and release.

Where do you begin? How will you navigate through life's tragedies? Without a purpose to keep you on course you'll end up wandering around hopelessly lost.

Take God's Word as a compass and our stories as signposts on the road to see the King.

THE STORY WITHIN
THE STORY

In the opening scene of the movie *The Princess Bride* the grandfather visits with his young grandson, who is playing a video game while sick in bed. He presents him a special gift—a book.

The book is the same book that was read to him and that he read to the boy's father when he was sick. When the grandpa says, "And today, I'm gonna read it to you," the boy appears disappointed and asks if there are any sports in it.

"Are you kidding? Fencing, fighting, torture, revenge, giants, monsters, chases, escapes, true love, miracles."[2] After receiving a *whatever* response, the old man goes on to tell the tale of the farm boy Westley and the Princess Buttercup.

The purpose of this fairy tale was to prove that true love cannot be broken. When she was in danger, the princess said to Prince Humperdink, "You can't hurt me. Westley and I are joined by the bonds of love, and you cannot track that; not with a thousand bloodhounds. And you cannot break it, not with a thousand swords."[3]

Classic stories like *The Princess Bride, Chicken Little, Lord of the Rings,* and *The Wizard of Oz* share a common motif—life is a perilous journey, filled with hidden meaning and great reward.

My wife and I recently celebrated our fortieth wedding anniversary. Life with Debbie has been an amazing journey full of beautiful, awe-inspiring moments. It is a tale of fearless love and surprising intrigue. We have cried tears of sorrow and tears of joy. It has been an unusual and exciting, sometimes hazardous adventure in trusting God.

There were times in the journey when darkness surrounded us and we couldn't move, nor see ahead. There were moments when God's voice was clear, but our courage to move forward was challenged. There were experiences we would have not chosen to go through—chapters we would have wished to never have been written.

Strangely, though, we learned this was all a part of God's plan. Each adversity proved his faithfulness so emphatically that we could tell our children and grandchildren that no matter what the circumstances and the fears that came with them, his ways can always be trusted.

How is this trust possible? Debbie and I are joined together with the eternal bonds of love—the steadfast love of the LORD—which cannot be broken.

God is a storyteller. He is telling a story about our lives. However, the story is about much more than the actions, thoughts, and feelings of the people involved. He is the main character. Each story is ultimately about him, and how he is drawing us to himself to trust him in all the uncertainties of life.

On the road to the Kingdom of Heaven we may experience doubt and confusion. Like Henny Penny, in the fairy tale *Chicken Little*, we may even feel as though the sky is falling and our world is coming to an end. What we don't realize in God's stories there is always something bigger going on—a spiritual understanding that changes everything for the better. *There is a story within the story!*

Now, let me prepare you. Before you enter into our story I encourage you to lay aside your presuppositions and get ready to stretch your thinking about God.

Why is that?

The Father, Son, and Holy Spirit got together to dream a story about our lives. The reader would anticipate the tales to be beautiful with a predictable, storybook ending.

However, we've found that God's stories can be told in the shadows, with the plot twisted and painful. At times he seems to be uncaring—even treasonable—as if the Trinity is throwing a party for evil.

What does all this mean? God is a benevolent conspirator.

Unbeknown to us, he is weaving good and evil together in his perfect plan, which is designed to reveal and accomplish his hidden purpose for our lives. He brilliantly uses our tragedies as opportunities for us to know the depth of his heart and that he has our best interests in mind.

What if he has purposefully placed the unwanted road hazards in our way to bring us to a place of complete reliance on him? This kind of unconditional trust frees us to walk the road he has designed specifically and uniquely for each of us to follow.

Life with God is an antinomy. That's when two irreconcilable forces work together to form an undeniable truth.

For example, in 2 Corinthians 12:9 the Apostle Paul uses the terms *weak* and *strong* to add depth and color to our journey with Christ. On their own, the two conditions are black and white, seemingly in opposition to each other. When united, they form an alliance of absolute power that enables us to walk (live) triumphantly.

Debbie and I have prayed many times for God to deliver us from evil. He very well could have. But, often he chose to answer our prayer with a *no* or *not now*. After a while we caught on. We came to realize this meant he had something better in store.

The truth is—experiencing his mercies under trying situations has been the best thing that ever happened to us. How else would we come to know God's grace is sufficient in every need? If he is not enough, that would make him untrustworthy.

One of the biggest lessons we've learned from God is that he may not be eager to rescue us from the overwhelming circumstances in which we may find ourselves. Instead, he might rather us continue to be weak, to take the winding road and discover a greater treasure.

In the *Lord of the Rings* J. R. R. Tolkien writes about two little hobbits who are on a journey to save the world. Sam turns to Frodo and says, "I wonder what sort of tale we've fallen into?"[4] Their journey is a story waiting to unfold. Something grand is about to happen.

Likewise, God's story for us is a purposeful journey. John Eldredge, the author of *Epic*, says we must take the journey to figure God out and the role he has for us.[5] We must bravely continue on, to know the rest of the story, so we can be an example for others to follow.

When God asked us to join him in his story, we wholeheartedly answered "Yes!" We've lived the stories you're about to encounter. In every situation we've been through, he has been faithful to our family, morning after morning, day after day, and year after year. We are eager to tell you about the God we know and why you should always trust in him, no matter what.

With God, you are destined to experience more adventure and wonder than you could have ever thought possible. Like the lion in *The Wizard of Oz*, you will need courage to face your fears. You will need faith to embrace the possibilities that God created just for you, as you discover the joy of trusting him!

When he invites you to join him in his story, how will you respond?

CHAPTER 1

First Faith

> I am reminded of your sincere faith, a faith
> that dwelt first in your grandmother Lois
> and your mother Eunice.
>
> —2 Timothy 1:5

Michael Erich McCrum was born on December 1, 1955, to parents Duane and Jean McCrum. My dad and mom were serving as missionary church planters on the Big Island of Hawaii. We lived in Honokaa, about forty miles north of Hilo and thirty miles east of Kona.

My memories include devouring juicy pineapples, sucking on sugar cane, swimming at Kawaihae Beach, and playing with my dog, Brownie. I also remember how difficult it was on my dad to see such little response to the gospel. When I turned six, we returned to the mainland for his next assignment with the mission agency.

I spent the next twelve years growing up in the foothills of southeast Missouri. The county seat and nearby town was Greenville, which had a population of 301. My father was chosen by Baptist Mid-Missions out of Cleveland, Ohio, to develop a missionary retirement village near the township of Silva, called Missionary Acres.

Life in the country offered a carefree environment that a boy dreams of having. Hot summer days usually included walking a mile barefoot to Elmo's Grocery Store, a rickety old building the size of a living room. My friends and I would scavenge for empty soda bottles in the ditch along the highway to return them for two cents each. I'd usually find enough bottles to buy a ten cent Frostie Root Beer and a five cent Zero candy bar.

It was normal to leave home in the morning and not return until supper time. There was so much for me and my friends to do, like walking dusty gravel roads that led nowhere. Along the way, we could catch crawdads in tiny streams, have dirt clod fights in a newly plowed field, sit in apple trees and eat apples until our stomachs ached, catch bullfrogs, and, if we were desperate enough, go swimming in the cow pond in our underwear. Or, we could always play baseball, using cow patties for bases!

If we behaved, our parents would drive us to the better swimming holes: Baker's Park, Black Bridge, and Bear Creek, where clear, refreshing water welcomed a running dive. We were surrounded by several rivers and lakes, and I loved going fishing with my grandfather, John McCrum. He also taught me how to water-ski on our two-acre lake.

I know I must have kept my guardian angels on edge. The lake on Missionary Acres would freeze over in winter, enough to walk or skate on. One day I was by myself on the lake. I tested the thickness of the ice by stomping with my foot. It seemed okay. I then got a running start from the bank and attempted to slidc thc two hundred feet across.

I was twenty feet from shore when the ice started to crack, and I broke through. Thankfully, the water was only five feet deep. I pushed off the bottom and the force lifted me back up on the ice. I slowly inched my way to shore. I was soaking wet—and freezing. I ran home and upstairs to the bathroom to change clothes before my parents ever knew what happened. I've thought about that day many times—the day I nearly drowned.

I was fortunate to attend White Hollow School, a one-room schoolhouse, and to have Mrs. Woods as my teacher. She inspired in me a love for reading, writing, and arithmetic. We looked forward to Friday afternoons when we'd end the week with a ciphering match (a math competition) on the chalkboard.

We had the best neighbors. Mrs. Emerson, an elderly woman who lived next door, would often walk over with a freshly baked custard pie. I don't know what I cnjoyed more—swallowing down a delicious slice or seeing the joy it brought to her beautifully weathered face.

Then there was Miss Grace Lamar, my Sunday school teacher. She was single and retired. The boys in her class thought she was mean and ugly. The truth was we were afraid of her.

One year I received a BB gun for Christmas. I hurriedly went outside, loaded BBs in the rifle, and scanned my surroundings. I locked in on a worthy target in the parking lot across the street— Miss Lamar's station wagon. I thought to myself, *I'll just make a nice dent in the side panel of her car.* I raised the gun, aimed, and pulled the trigger. To my amazement, I shattered the entire back window!

My dad made me go to Miss Lamar's house to say that I was sorry. The two-hundred-yard walk to her mobile home seemed like a death march. There was no doubt in my mind—she was going to kill me. I cried all the way to her front door step.

Then, to my surprise, she opened the door with a tender smile. Before I could get the words "I'm sorry" out of my mouth, she reached out to me with open arms and drew me close. "Oh Mike, I love you, and I forgive you."

What? Was I mistaken about Miss Lamar? That was the last thing I expected. I didn't realize it then, but I realize it now: the grace I received from Grace was the grace of God.

I became good friends with Grace Lamar. She kept up with how God was leading me. Every time I would come home from college, she would come up to me in church and smile, reach out her arms like she did that Christmas day, and hug me. She was the embodiment of grace and taught me a lesson I've asked God to reproduce in my life.

My grandmother, Thelma, and my mother, Jean, had the greatest influence on my early life. Like Lois and Eunice in the Bible, they were the first to instill in me their faith in God.

In the early 1930s, my grandparents settled in Taylor, Michigan. The story goes that Grandma McCrum became convicted about how their drinking and worldly lifestyles were affecting their four children.[6]

One Sunday while Grandma was getting four-year-old Duane (my dad) ready for Sunday school, he cried out, "You don't go!" To which she responded, "I'll start going to church the first of the year."

Grandma McCrum kept her promise—a resolution that was never broken. Mrs. Forrest Friend, a church member at Evangel Baptist Church, made her feel welcome, and the Word of God began to take effect.

That year the family attended a revival. The speaker was Reverend Wapato, a Native American evangelist. It seems that Granddad McCrum was so convicted that he jumped out of his seat and went down to the front before the invitation song even started. As a result, the Lord restored the entire family—and that's when the McCrum spiritual legacy began.

***

I trusted Jesus Christ as my Savior on May 8, 1963. I was attending a youth meeting in the basement of our home when I heard my father speak on heaven and hell. I particularly listened to what he said about hell. I was afraid that I was going there.

When the invitation was given to receive God's gift of eternal life, I went forward. My grandmother met me and took me upstairs to my bedroom. We sat on the edge of my bed while she read about the road to salvation in Romans.

> None is righteous—no not one. (3:10)

> All have sinned and fallen short of the glory of God. (3:23)

> The wages of sin is death, but the free gift of God is eternal life. (6:23)

> Everyone who calls on the name of the Lord will be saved. (10:9)

She prayed and then invited me to pray. I knelt beside my bed, confessed that I was a sinner, and received Jesus Christ into my life. It was that simple. I was seven years old and couldn't wait to tell my friends at school about the decision I had made. The following year I was baptized by my father in the Black River, near Poplar Bluff, Missouri.

I learned about helping the needy from Grandma McCrum. She found out about some poor families near White Hollow. Faithfully, each week she would buy groceries and take clothes to them. She was a faithful missionary to them for several years—until her health declined. Incredibly, her ministry has sparked four generations of missionaries!

My mother was simple, graceful, beautiful, and faithful. One thing unique about her was that she only had an eighth-grade education. Mom became a

Christian in her youth. And even though she was not looking to become a missionary, she joyfully served with her mission board until she was sixty-five. She raised four children and nurtured us through some very trying moments.

One day when I was in high school, she came into my bedroom and sat at the foot of my bed to talk. In tenderness she said, "I've heard about what you've been up to. The neighbor told me. You can continue with what you're doing, but most likely it will end up hurting you—and not only you, but your family."

My mother became a model of courage and conveyed to me that, despite my rebellious ways, my life was important to God. Sometimes when I would come home late at night, I could see through the crack in her bedroom door that she was on her knees praying.

Later on, I asked my mom if she had prayed for me during those difficult teenage years. She smiled and said, "Son, I've prayed for you every day of your life." There's no doubt that it was the prayers of my mom that got me through.

Her favorite verse in the Bible was Joshua 1:9.

> Have not I commanded you? Be strong and courageous. Do not be frightened, and do not be dismayed, for the LORD your God is with you wherever you go.

My mom gave me a huge gift. She taught me that I can always trust in God, no matter what. This was especially true of her after what happened to Dad.

CHAPTER 2

The Accident

Only one life, 'twill soon be past. Only what's done for Christ will last.

—C. T. Studd

The summer of 1969 was monumental—for two reasons. On July 20th Apollo 11 landed on the moon. Astronaut Neil Armstrong became the first human to step on the moon's surface. He uttered the now historical words: "One small step for man, one giant leap for mankind."

I remember that moment very well because while that was going on, my two friends and I had broken into a neighbor's house and happened to turn the TV on to see the news. We made a mess of things and stole some items. We thought we would hide the goods in the basement of the church across the street. Not smart.

A month later a deacon in the church discovered the items and told my father. The church board asked my dad and me to meet with them before a Wednesday night prayer meeting. This made things difficult because my father was the pastor of the church.

During my interrogation, I peeked over at my dad. I could tell by the look on his face that he was greatly disappointed in his thirteen-year-old son. When I couldn't take it anymore, I bolted from my seat and ran straight home to my bedroom, where I cried myself to sleep.

***

Dad married my mom when she was sixteen. He felt the call of God on his life and received training from Detroit Bible College. After serving a tour of military duty in the Philippines, he and Mom joined Baptist Mid-Missions and were appointed as missionaries to Hawaii.

Following eight years of church planting in Honokaa, they were asked by the mission to develop Missionary Acres in Missouri. He sacrificed his life to carve out a thriving missionary retirement village from one hundred and twenty dense, mountainous acres. He built roads, houses, and maintenance buildings, dug through hard pan soil to lay water and sewer lines, formed a small lake, and constructed nice homes for those returning after years of missionary service.

It seemed there was no limit to what he could do. Once he salvaged an old, rusty Caterpillar road grader. He took the entire grader apart, rebuilt the engine, and painted it. It ran like new. He also chiseled out the wooden Missionary Acres sign that people still see from the highway.

Driving a tractor and working with a back hoe took a heavy toll on his back. He visited his chiropractor every Saturday morning. Despite the daily pain, he would work long, hard days, coming home for supper and then going directly to bed. He loved the ministry that much.

My dad was well known in the communities where he served and was respected by many. He would plant three churches in his lifetime: Honokaa Baptist Church in Hawaii, Evangel Baptist Church at Missionary Acres, and New Testament Baptist Church in Poplar Bluff, Missouri.

***

During breakfast the next morning there was a cold, ominous silence. Nothing was said about the results from the meeting and what would happen to me. But, the woeful concern in my father's eyes conveyed grave sadness. I could only imagine the worst—*Because of what you've done, I am resigning the church. My ministry is over.*

For the next three days we didn't talk to each other. Then on Saturday morning, September 6th, he said he wanted me to mow the yard. I promised I would, but never got around to it. Instead, I lay on the couch and watched TV all day.

When it was supper time, my mother asked me to go check on my dad and let him know dinner was ready. I came up with the excuse that I was too tired to go. She went to the garage, instead.

In a few moments I heard my mom scream. Running inside, she shouted, "Son, something terrible has happened to your father! Hurry, call the neighbors!"

My heart was pounding like a jack hammer. When Dotty Seldon answered the phone I blurted out, "I think my dad is dead!"

I ran out to the garage to see for myself. Apparently, while changing the oil underneath his car, the jack slipped and the car fell on my dad. I tried to free him, but it was no use—he was gone. Distraught, I started throwing boxes, tools, anything I could get my hands on, all over the garage. In a matter of minutes neighbors were gathered around, frantically trying to raise the car.

One of them took me to their house, where I laid on the master bed for hours, crying my heart out. Fear filled my mind. What would it be like to be without a dad? As far as I was concerned, the world had come to an end.

My father lived a very full forty-one years. He frequently quoted from a poem written by C. T. Studd, one of the Cambridge Seven, who in 1885 offered themselves to Hudson Taylor for missionary service with the China Inland Mission. Later, Studd would ignore medical advice and serve in the Belgian Congo and India. His motto was "Only one life, 'twill soon be past. Only what's done for Christ will last."[7]

For a good part of my life I felt that I had caused my dad's death. The words, *Because of what you've done,* kept reverberating in my head. I longed to talk to my father and say I was sorry. I tried to hide my pain through performance. I turned to sports and my peers for love and acceptance, but was never satisfied.

Something was missing. Over time I learned that when I lost my dad, I lost the one thing that a son needed most from his father—intimacy. I needed to know that I was loved. I needed closeness, the assurance that I belonged to him...and that he believed in me!

How would I survive? God was faithful. He surrounded me with some men who built into my life and encouraged me. They included Buck Rhodes, my high school basketball coach, Bill Hollida, the father of my girlfriend, Charles Barker, my high school principal, and George Ward, my Industrial Arts instructor. My brothers, Larry and Roger, also looked out for me.

But, the person I watched and learned from the most was my mother. I marveled how, in spite of losing her husband, she trusted in God and relied on him to meet her every need. Her daily smile was an affirmation of his faithfulness, assuring me that somehow everything would be okay.

***

Trusting in Christ for eternal life and obeying his will was one thing, but trusting Christ with upsetting situations and fatal events was another. This was all new to me.

I began to realize that in spite of the incredible pain left over from my dad's death, there was something bigger going on. I like to think that God was drawing me to himself—to provide the intimacy my soul was crying out for. This was a story waiting to unfold. My goal became to discover the rest of the story.

It seemed that what happened to my father was mysteriously planned by the Trinity as a part of my journey to the King. The path would lead through great pain. According to Frederick Buechner, American writer and theologian, the question facing me would be, "Will I be a good steward of it?"[8]

Over time, pain would become my friend. I would see hurt, sorrow, suffering, thorns, weakness, and calamity as valuable treasures. I've learned that these can be sacred moments and integral parts of our journey. Instead of being apprehensive and fearing them, I needed to embrace them. God desires to help us triumph through life's tragedies.

We're tempted to hide pain from ourselves, our family, the world, even God. We can try burying it or seeing it as an excuse for failure. However, Jesus wants us to invest it for his sake, and the sake of others.

In the Gospel of Matthew he tells a story about a man going on a journey who entrusted all his property to his servants. When the man returned he settled his accounts and rewarded his servants according to how they invested their talents. Those who made the right investment were rewarded.

The same is true of us. If we accept and redeem the life Jesus ordained for us, then we'll someday hear these words: "Well done, good and faithful servant. You have been faithful over a few things,

I will make you ruler over many things" (Matthew 25:23).

Something may happen that could stop us dead in our tracks. That's a divine opportunity in disguise, even when things go wrong, to deepen our faith and become more dependent on God. His ways are not always understandable, but they are always to be trusted.

Our story may not turn out as we had hoped it would. Knowing God walks with us "through the valley of the shadow of death," allows us to "fear no evil," for he is with us (Psalm 23:4).

CHAPTER 3

Sawmill Revival

Mike, no one ever told me about this before.
—Pat Bennett

The two things that mattered most to me in high school were my girlfriend Marty and playing basketball. I always thought I'd marry my high school sweetheart, and my secret dream was to do something that, to my knowledge, no one from Greenville High School had ever accomplished—play college basketball.

My two older brothers were varsity players and I got to ride on the player's bus to varsity games and watch them play. I soon became addicted to the sport. I'd listen to local basketball games broadcast on the radio during the regional tournaments, and dream about what it would be like to be on a team that went to the state championship.

My brother Larry played forward and Roger played guard. One day during their practice the coach let me join the players in a shoot around. The guys referred to Larry as Big Mac and Roger as Middle Mac. I became Little Mac.

I couldn't wait until it was my turn. I played junior varsity and varsity with Randy Montgomery, Jeff White, Steve Stroup, Ron Porter, Randy Shell, Dennis Ross, Pat Bennett, Louis McLean, Eric Walker, and Monty Tidwell. We won a few sectional tournaments, but each season would end abruptly on the way to state.

I stayed after school and played ball for hours. Running laps or suicide drills during team practice never seemed a hardship to me. I just loved racing down the court and enjoyed every minute. That's about all I did during the season—eat, sleep, eat some more, and play basketball.

When I wasn't playing, I'd have my eye on the TV, watching Pistol Pete Maravich play for Louisiana State University. He would score most of the points for his team, while leaving the opponent mesmerized with his ability to dribble behind his back and make long jump shots. I'd practice by myself for hours trying to copy his shot, even sporting his definitive loose basketball socks, hoping it would make me play just like him!

I loved it when Coach Rhodes would say during a game time out, "Guys, I want you to run the *cack* out of the ball!" I never knew where he came up with that word, but it meant to fast break, score, do a full court press, and run the other team out of the gymnasium. Many times we did just that.

When not playing basketball, I would be at Bill and Shirley Hollida's large Charolaise cattle farm, hanging out with Marty. I often helped the family haul and stack bales of hay in their large red barn. One year I painted their "Rocking H" logo on the front of it.

Every Fourth of July families would gather at the City Park in Greenville to celebrate Independence Day. Among the various festivities was the annual pie eating contest. One year the featured dessert was chocolate pie. Since that was my favorite, I decided to participate. I remember forcing down pie after pie until I was ready to throw up. It was a long time before I could even look at a chocolate pie.

During my freshman year at GHS, I would often act out in class and be sent to the principal's office. Come to think of it, I'm sure I was still reeling from my dad's death and I didn't know how to cope with such loss.

I probably wouldn't have gotten serious about life had it not been for Mr. Barker and the time his discipline brought an end to my poor behavior. It was his memorable words that helped point me in the right direction: "Mr. McCrum, you are better than this. If you don't change your behavior, you'll never become anything!" From that day forward he continued to have a positive impact on my life and we became good friends.

Even though our high school only had around two hundred students, Mr. Ward was hired to set up an impressive industrial arts program with state-of-the-art machinery. My junior year I built a stereo cabinet. My senior year I crafted a dining room hutch. Both of these are in our home today.

My pride and joy were my cars: a white 1961 Ford Falcon and a blue 1963 Ford Galaxy. I put a lot of sweat into making them run and look nice. Somehow, my older brother Larry convinced me to sell the Galaxy for $300. As the buyer drove the car away, he promised to pay me later. I haven't seen him, or his money, since!

Our senior class was made up of forty students. For our senior trip, Mr. Ward and Mrs. Sue Barker took us to Washington, DC, New York City, and Niagara Falls. Most of the class had never been out of the state of Missouri.

When it came time for me to go away to college, I tried to stay as close as I could to home to be near Marty. I enrolled in Baptist Bible College in Springfield, Missouri in the fall of 1973. I worked hard at my sport and it paid off—I made the freshman basketball team.

I was on the way to fulfilling my dream, when I suddenly came to a fork in the road. To the left the way was wide open and inviting. Many were taking that road. One billboard was especially luring to me. It flashed "The Thrill of Basketball."

The road to the right, however, looked narrow, twisted, and somewhat foreboding. Not many people were headed that way. The sign over it read, "God's School."

According to Gene Edwards, the narrow road is the road to God's University.[9] God's school is a small school. Not very many men and women apply to attend. Few graduate. The reason is because his university is a school of brokenness. All who enroll must suffer pain. Someone, something seemed to draw me to the right like a giant magnet.

In October the Jack Van Impe Crusade came to our college campus. Out of curiosity I decided to attend an evening service. It was during that meeting that I sensed God might be calling me into ministry.

Earth's passions and playing basketball began to take on lesser meaning. A few days later I met a fellow student named Ron Miller. He was a gifted basketball player, much better than me. I asked him why he hadn't tried out for the team. His answer was to invite me to grab my tennis shoes and follow him.

What I experienced with Ron that day would change my perspective on the future. He took me to the inner city, where we joined in to play basketball with the kids. After the game he pulled out his pocket-size New Testament and began witnessing to the guys. I watched in amazement as they all listened, and some prayed to receive Christ as Savior.

As I went to bed that night I started thinking about the guys I had played basketball with back at Greenville High School. I had never told them about Christ. The next day I asked Ron if he would come with me and go back home to share the gospel with them. We did more than that. As it turned out, we went back to hold a youth revival!

Returning home on a November Saturday, we drove around trying to find some of my teammates. But strangely enough, none could be found. We tried one more place—the sawmill behind Randy Montgomery's house. When we walked into the mill, I was happy to see Randy and Pat Bennett, along with four of my school friends.

After shutting down the saws and machinery, they gathered around and I told them why we were there. I said we had come to tell them about Jesus. To my amazement one by one they made their way toward Ron and me.

Randy had been our most valuable player. Ron opened his New Testament and prayed with him. He was the first to trust in Christ.

Pat was one of the forwards on our team. After I prayed with him, he looked at me and with tears in his eyes said, "Mike, no one ever told me about this before." By the time we left, all six prayed to receive Christ!

It was at that sawmill that Jesus made his direction clear—he wanted me to share the gospel full time.

I decided to leave the basketball team and I transferred to Tennessee Temple College in Chattanooga in January 1974, where I could focus on preparing for vocational ministry.

Marty and I found it difficult to maintain a long-distance relationship, and so we parted ways.

Dr. Lee Roberson and Dr. J. R. Faulkner were chancellor and vice president at the college. The school was abuzz with activity, having an enrollment of over two thousand students. I was impacted by Dr. Roberson's compassionate leadership. He was the first one I heard to make the statement, "Everything rises or falls on leadership."

My years at Temple were profound and revealing. I realized that I couldn't walk the journey alone.

I needed a life-long companion, a trusted partner, one with whom I could share my dreams. I needed someone who could experience with me the amazing, transformative power that is generated by two lives coming together in Christ.

I needed a true friend to encourage me, to help get me back on my feet when I stumble and fall. I needed someone to always be there with me, sharing the pain and the pleasure, and living in the healing and the blessing.

But, who was it the King had prepared to walk the journey with me, to travel the road of ministry together? It was in the middle of my sophomore year that the answer became clear.

CHAPTER 4

Cinderella

Don't date Mike! He's going to be a missionary to tribal people.

—Debbie's Friends

It was January 5, 1975. I had just returned to campus from two weeks of Christmas break. All the students were due back for spring semester and were expected to attend the Sunday evening campus worship service.

When the service was over I started to make my way over to the aisle, and there she was, standing ten feet away—the most beautiful woman I'd ever seen. *Wow!* I thought, *Who is she?* I hadn't seen her before on campus, and if I didn't act now, then chances of finding her would be all but gone.

I hurriedly tried to squeeze down the crowded pew, stepping all over people to get to the aisle. But when I got there, the angel in the green dress was gone.

Frantic, I maneuvered my way through the crowd and made it to the foyer. That's when I caught a glimpse of Cinderella, stepping outside. There was no time to plan my approach, so when I caught up with her, I looked into her beautiful face and said, "Hi! Isn't your name Linda?"

It was a clumsy way to start a conversation, but she kindly smiled and said, "No, my name is Debbie." When I saw her smile and say her name I knew she was the one I would marry.

I walked the two blocks with her to her dorm. I felt pretty good about myself, since I knew girls at our Bible college considered getting walked home from church a quarter of a date. I learned everything I could about her in ten minutes. I raced back to my dorm room, looked her up in the yearbook, and then announced to my roommates that I found the woman who would become my wife!

The next day I phoned Debbie, hoping to ask her to go with me to the campus basketball game. I prayed, "Lord, when I call and she comes to the phone and says she'd love to go, I'll know that it's a sign that she's truly the one you meant for me." Well, she came to the phone, we went to the game together, and the rest is history.

***

DEBBIE: *Debra Deane Ferrell was born in Panama City, Florida, on February 13, 1955. I was the oldest of six girls. My father, Hubert Ferrell, worked hard as a conductor for the Bay Line Railroad. Olive Ferrell was a mother and fabulous homemaker.*

I was not born into a Christian home. My parents were from good, moral families, but didn't attend church much after adolescence.

My father worked with a man named Harold Richardson, who consistently invited him to church. He finally attended with my mom and they soon gave their lives to Christ.

Over the years, Mother and Daddy tried several times a week to get us all together after dinner for Bible reading and prayer. It was after one of those family devotional times that my father said to me, "Debbie, Mommy and I are going to heaven when we die. Are you?" I tearfully replied, "No."

Daddy read some scriptures about how to ask Jesus into my heart. I will never forget that night. I was about seven years old when I prayed to receive Christ as my Savior.

I was blessed to grow up attending Central Baptist Church, where the pastor was Dr. Hugh Pyle. The first church services were held in an old airplane hangar before the new sanctuary was built. I had wonderful parents who made sure that I was there every time the doors were open. We were also faithful attenders at Sunday school class every Sunday morning before the worship service.

I could hardly wait to one day be in Mrs. Pyle's fourth-grade girls' class. Everyone loved her. Being in her Sunday school class was wonderful and from that point on all I wanted to be when I grew up was a pastor's wife.

Mrs. Pyle was always so kind. I noticed she would often have people or out-of-town guests in her home for meals. That looked like such fun to me. It's something I enjoy to this day as a pastor's wife.

When I was fifteen years old, our pastor preached a sermon entitled, "Giving God Your Life." He challenged the congregation to be willing to let God guide you as you decided what to do with your life.

After the sermon he asked anyone who wanted to take the challenge to come stand at the front of the church and he would pray for them. I went and so did my best friend, Linda. From that time on I really felt God was leading me into ministry.

When I was seventeen, I visited Tennessee Temple College and left thinking that was where I wanted to attend college. I hoped to meet someone there who would help me fulfill my dream of being a pastor's wife.

As I left for school on August 31, 1973, I was both excited and sad. I was excited because I was living my dream of going to a Christian college and sad because I was leaving my sweet family. I would miss my parents, but I would especially miss my five sisters.

Patti was sixteen, Peggy twelve, Becky nine, Missy six, and little Susie was only three years old. I felt that by leaving them I would miss watching them grow up.

College was great! I made a lot of friends and I loved my studies. I lived mostly for Christmas and summer breaks. At the end of each school year I would go home to my part-time job, hoping the summer would never end. When the time came, I hated to say goodbye again.

The fall semester of my sophomore year I felt God prodding me to examine my relationship with my boyfriend back home. He was a nice guy who loved Jesus, attended the local college, and would make a fine husband. I was feeling more and more a call to ministry, but it was a bit confusing, because I didn't have any idea what ministry God had in mind.

By the time I went home for Christmas break in 1974, I knew what I must do: end my relationship with my boyfriend. He was a great person, but we simply were headed down two different paths.

I returned to college in early January 1975, vowing to never date again. Boys were so much trouble and I was really into my studies. But, God had other plans.

I met Mike only two days after returning to school. We began to date and quickly fell in love. Dating while at Bible college was so much fun. There were always sporting events, concerts, and plenty of other things to do together.

Mike planned to end up on the mission field. Several of my friends warned me: "Don't date Mike! He's going to be a missionary to tribal people." This bothered me, because at the time missions was the only type of ministry that I really didn't want to participate in. However, I figured that I'd cross that bridge later.

My hesitation wasn't because I thought missions was unimportant. Missions and missionaries have always been important to me. I remember the first missionary that I ever saw. I was about eight years old and we were having a special missions service at our church. One missionary who came for the week *had an orphanage in Mexico. He actually brought a little Mexican boy with him and I remember he wore a poncho and a sombrero. I couldn't stop staring at him.*

I told God when I was fifteen, that I would do ministry if he wanted me to, but I really didn't want to be a missionary. I was afraid he'd call me to Japan or the jungle. The jungle seemed too scary and it takes so long to learn Japanese—why, they don't even use our alphabet.

***

While Debbie and I were dating we would often attend FMF (Foreign Missions Fellowship) which met on campus every evening at 5:55 p.m. The meetings were *the* place to be. Student leader Don Bryant would usually give a brief challenge from the Bible and then share updates on what God was doing around the world. This was followed by a time of prayer in groups of two.

It was at these gatherings that Debbie and I were drawn closer together. While attending, we began to develop an intimate trust between ourselves and God. This time meant so much to us. We agreed if we were to ever marry, we would start our wedding ceremony at 5:55 p.m.

CHAPTER 5

5:55 P.M.

No eye has seen a God beside you, who acts for those who wait for him.

—Isaiah 64:4

The more Debbie and I dated and got to know each other, the more it became clear—God wanted us to share the future together. Now it was time for me to meet her parents. I thought maybe this would be the time to ask her to marry me, while visiting her home in Florida on an April weekend.

I made it a point to get to know Mr. and Mrs. Ferrell and Debbie's five sisters. I was impressed with the way her mom and dad had raised their family. I imagined what being married to Debbie would be like.

The two of us spent Saturday afternoon walking the beach on the Gulf of Mexico. The gleaming stretches of pure white sand, the emerald-green waters, and the dunes with sea oats waving in the gentle breeze were staggering. Yet, nothing in God's creation could be more impressive than Debbie.

When I proposed to her on Sunday evening, April 13, 1975, she said, "Yes!" We were so excited! This was a dream come true.

However, our joy wasn't fully complete. We knew we had to tell her parents and seek their permission to marry before we drove back to school the next morning, because once we were on campus, the whole world would know. We stayed up the rest of the night, sitting on the couch, planning how we would ask her parents.

When Debbie's father got up at 4:00 a.m. to get ready for work, we knew the moment had arrived. We joined him and her mom at the breakfast table and with eyes half open, choked down a bowl of cold cereal.

I was shivering in my boots as I gathered up my courage to begin the conversation. I told Mr. and Mrs. Ferrell how much I had enjoyed meeting them and thanked them for allowing me to date their daughter. I then shared that we had fallen in love and that we would like their permission to get married.

There was a long moment of silence. I could tell by the expression on their face that I had caught them off guard and didn't know what to say. When Debbie came and stood by my side, her presence was like the calm in the eye of a storm. Finally, her dad spoke up and said, "We'll have to think about it."

Looking back, Debbie and I wonder if things could have been handled better. (Like, I didn't know the importance of asking the parent's permission first.) I was definitely caught up in the moment and insensitive to the desires of those around me.

Debbie had wished we could have finished college before getting married. When she realized I wanted to get married within the year, she had to really think about it. I know now that this put her in a difficult situation, whether to honor her parents or follow my lead.

We drove the eight hours back to college. When I entered my dorm room, my roommate Rick Ragan (later, my best man) took one look at me and knew something was up. My smile was a dead giveaway. To celebrate, they threw me into the men's shower. Debbie had similar results in her dorm, and it wasn't long before the news had made it across campus.

At the end of the week we called her parents and they reluctantly gave us permission to marry. After all, we had only met a few months earlier. We chose August 15th as our wedding day...only four months away.

Later, Debbie and I went out for dinner to celebrate. Our favorite place to eat was at Los Charros Mexican restaurant at the base of Lookout Mountain in Chattanooga. I told her I wanted to take her to a nearby park to see a large rock I had found. I arranged with one of my professors to come and take a picture as we stood beside the huge bolder. That's when I happily presented Debbie an engagement ring.

DEBBIE: *Now, forty years later, I look back on our first few months of marriage and remember how hard it was to combine homemaking and college studies. But we were so much in love and so happy to be married. Next to Jesus, Mike is the best thing that ever happened to me.*

***

During the summer, before we were married, I traveled for the college playing the character of Jim Elliot in a drama called *Bridge of Blood,* written by David Robey. I toured with nine other students to churches around the South presenting the drama almost every day. In the meantime, Debbie was at home preparing for our wedding.

A passage of Scripture that had come to mean a lot to us was Isaiah 64:4. We decided to have it engraved inside our wedding bands. The verse says: "No eye has seen a God beside you, who acts for those who wait for him."

From the start, we both expected to see amazing things happen because we had waited on him to bring us the right person to marry. We began to dream a dream together. We believed that our marriage was what God wanted in order to give him the most glory.

While I was on tour, it was at one of those churches in Hueytown, Alabama, that I met Fritz and Joyce Harter. They had been missionaries to the primitive Yanomamo Indians in Brazil, South America. Their ministry was cut short and they had to return when Joyce had health issues.

After the performance a couple of us spent the night in their home. For me, it was to be one of those divine appointments the Lord uses in our lives. We stayed up for hours looking at pictures and listening to them talk about their jungle ministry.

The next day I wrote Debbie a letter and told her about my experience with the Harters. I disclosed that they were praying for a couple to take their place. When she read the letter she thought this could be where God was leading us to minister. It confirmed what I knew in my heart...that Debbie and I were that couple.

***

How do we know God's calling? I believe his will for us is found in Jesus' words given in Matthew 28:18-20. The call is simple and clear—to make disciples of all nations. Dr. Crawford Loritts recently preached on what Jesus had in mind for his followers:

> The great commission in Matthew 28:18-20 represents the purpose of the Christian life...Based on Genesis 1 we are the image bearers of God in others, and making disciples is what we do...Everyone has received a call to discipleship. It is simply a matter of obedience.[10]

We knew God had called us to make disciples and he placed Fritz and Joyce in our path to make us aware of the opportunity to do that among the Yanomamo. We volunteered to go in the name of the King and bare witness of the transformation in our lives.

In a way, going to the jungle was out of our comfort zone, but Jesus gives us the desire, the spiritual gifts, and the power to be witnesses for him, no matter where. Besides, he had *asked* us to go.

I answered the call to please the King, not for significance or man's applause. If I wanted that, then I would have taken the sports route. Dr. Loritts would say, "The call to ministry is not an occupation, rather it's an *obsession* to obey Christ and bring as many as we can to the kingdom." We go to declare God's glory to whomever he puts in front of us, be it the neighbor across the street or tribal people in Brazil.

Jim Elliot, missionary to Ecuador, once wrote, "We don't need a call. We need a kick in the pants!"[11]

***

Debbie and I were married on Friday evening, August 15th at Central Baptist Church in Panama City. Dr. Milton Ker performed the ceremony, and yes, it started at 5:55 p.m. I was nineteen and Debbie was twenty.

I couldn't believe my eyes when I saw Debbie walking down the aisle. Wow, I was a blessed man! We wrote our own vows and quoted several passages of Scripture to each other. It was a beautiful, sacred ceremony.

This was the best day of my life—the day Debbie said, "I do."

We spent our honeymoon back in Missouri where I grew up. On the way we surprised the Harters by showing up at their Sunday worship service in Hueytown. They invited us to their house for lunch and we talked about our future. That's when I announced to Debbie and the Harters that I felt Brazil was where God was calling us.

We went back to college for our junior and senior years. I had scholarships to cover my school bill as a result of traveling for the school. A student wife could attend for $300 a semester. I promised her dad that Debbie would graduate. And we did, together, on August 11, 1977, both with Bachelor of Science degrees.

During those first few years of marriage we lived from week to week. Debbie found a part-time job at a fabric store. My brother, Roger, had just graduated from Temple's seminary and gave me his job at a picture frame shop. We made enough money to cover groceries, utilities, gas, and pay $22 a week rent for the upstairs portion of an old house on Union Avenue, a half mile walk from campus.

One time it came to the end of the month and after paying the bills, there was no money to buy groceries. For a few days we ate Sugar Pops cereal for our meals, once without milk, just water.

Then, one night we heard a knock on the door. Doug Harper, a former college roommate, came by to visit. He soon noticed there was no food around. He smiled and said, "Get your keys. We're going grocery shopping!"

I don't think we fully appreciated it then, but we do now. God was faithful and provided for us time and time again. On more than one occasion we prayed for a specific financial need and God provided the exact amount...at the perfect time.

We began to learn by experience what it meant to depend on God for our day-to-day needs. This would be vitally necessary as we took a giant leap into full-time ministry.

CHAPTER 6

Jungle Bound

He is no fool, who gives what he cannot
keep, to gain what he cannot lose.
—Jim Elliot

On January 8, 1956, Jim Elliot, along with four
other missionary men, was killed by Auca Indians
on the Curaray River in Ecuador. It was a story
heard around the world. The article in *Life* magazine
read "Go into all the world and preach the gospel.
Five do, and die."[12]

Many called it "a purposeless nightmare of
tragedy." Understandable, since these young
men were in their twenties with wives and young
children. But, God had other plans. As a result
of this unbelievable story of self-sacrifice, a
countless number of people were moved to become
missionaries—my parents included.

I spent a lot of time reading about Jim and felt
the pull to try to follow in his footsteps. That's why

my visit with Fritz and Joyce was so exciting. Debbie and I would be serving in a similar situation.

When we said our marriage vows little did we know that this would mean taking up our cross to follow Christ—a journey that at times would be fearful, challenging, and painful. Our decision from the start was to trust him, no matter what. We truly believed that there was so much more to gain.

In the summer of 1976, we found ourselves in Philadelphia, Pennsylvania, attending candidate school with Unevangelized Fields Mission (UFM). Rev. Al Larson and Rev. Charlie Piepgrass were president and vice president, respectively. We would listen for hours as Al and his wife, Carol, told stories of their service in the former Belgian Congo in Central Africa, stories that included coming close to death on several occasions.

We were appointed as missionaries to Brazil on July 2, 1976. Debbie pointed out to me that this was the official date two hundred years before when the *Declaration of Independence* was signed. The actual celebration came on the 4th.

I was ordained into the gospel ministry and commissioned with Debbie at Central Baptist Church on August 15th of that year. Another couple was ordained the same evening—Jerry and Debbie Walls. Jerry now serves as pastor of Southside Baptist Church, a large church in Warner Robins, Georgia. Debbie's sister, Peggy Nash, and her husband, Randall, serve on staff at the church.

Following graduation from college, Debbie and I traveled to several churches to speak about our calling and to raise the required $800 a month financial support for Brazil. The first missionary conference we attended was at Shenandoah Baptist Church in Roanoke, Virginia.

At the close of the conference Senior Pastor Bob Alderman asked to have breakfast with me. As we were eating he said, "I don't know if this is crazy or not, but would you and Debbie pray about moving here to be our youth pastor until you leave for Brazil?"

Without hesitation, I said, "Pastor, there are some things we don't need to pray about. The answer is 'Yes!'" Afterward, I discussed our conversation with Debbie and she wholeheartedly agreed.

Shenandoah became our home church. We fell in love with the families, and the youth we served. While there our youth performed the drama *Bridge of Blood*. From that youth group at least two ended up in full-time ministry.

We also became close with Rev. John Fletcher at Faith Bible Church in Sterling, Virginia. When we attended a missionary conference there we learned that many of the members worked in Washington, DC. It was encouraging to us to see how many Christians were in government.

On May 13, 1978, Destiny Lynn McCrum was born in nearby Salem, Virginia. People asked us if we were planning on taking our baby to Brazil. Of course we were! However, both of us being twenty-two years old, we didn't appreciate how difficult the separation would be for grandparents and close friends. It was especially hard for Debbie.

We were eager to go to Brazil, even though the country wasn't granting permanent visas to US citizens at the time. We agreed to go with thirteen other missionaries on temporary (tourist) visas and apply for permanent residency from within the country.

On August 21, 1978, Debbie, three-month old Destiny, and I flew to Brazil to begin language school in Belém (Portuguese for Bethlehem).

My mom and dad had prayed their children would grow up to be missionaries. And, God was faithful to answer their prayers, beginning with Roger, and his wife Darlene, who planted churches in South Africa. Then, Debbie and I answered God's call to go to Brazil. Later, Larry, and his wife Delores, would serve in Hawaii and Sharon, and her husband Billy, would minister in Jamaica.

***

Belém was a bustling city located at the mouth of the Amazon River. During our eight months there we attended Portuguese language school and began to learn the culture of the people to whom we would be ministering.

We were able to witness to some of the young people coming by our compound to learn English. Two of them were Eliphaz and Ricardo. Eliphaz was named after one of Job's three friends in the Bible. Ricardo was the son of a Brazilian airline pilot. Both young men were always smiling and a delight to have in our home. They loved to hold Destiny, our little Portuguese *crianca* (small child). The highlight of our time with them came the day Ricardo gave his life to Christ.

We finished language school in April, 1979, and flew Varig Airlines to Roraima, the most northern territory of Brazil. From there we flew an additional two hundred and fifty miles interior on a single prop Cessna airplane piloted by Missionary Aviation Fellowship to Mucajai (Moo-kah-zhy-ee) station, where we would receive two weeks of jungle training with Steve and Dawn Anderson.

Our first night in the jungle we were kept awake all night long by small frogs chirping and jumping all over our bedroom. This must have been what it was like for the Egyptians leading up to the exodus! The next day, a challenging moment came for Debbie when she got to experience her first canoe ride through rapids...while holding Destiny on her lap!

On the morning of May 8, 1979, MAF flew us to Palimi-U (Pah-duh-me-oo) station where we set up a temporary home in Bob and Gay Cable's house, while they were on furlough in the States. Finally, we were at our long-awaited destination—the place and people God had put on our hearts to serve. The Yanomamo tribe we would be ministering to was related to the primitive Auca Indians among whom Jim and Elisabeth Elliot served in Ecuador.

Soon after our arrival the Indian men began to chop down palm trees along the river to make slats to build our house. Our modest jungle home had a tin roof with a fifty-five gallon drum to catch rain water for drinking and bathing. We had an outhouse for a bathroom. It was a distinct feature I had become accustomed to at White Hollow School in Missouri.

Dick Swain flew in from Boa Vista to help me construct our new jungle home. After retiring, he and his wife Lois moved to Brazil to assist missionaries. That put them near their daughter, Carol Swain, a single missionary at Mucajai. Dick had a flare for starting work before dawn. Often, he'd start up his chainsaw to wake us up.

Meanwhile, we began to learn the tribal language, which came easier for me than Portuguese. There were fewer letters in their alphabet and fewer words in their dialect. The Indians were very dramatic, often sucking in their chest or rolling on the ground to get the meaning of a word across.

Our two coworkers were Sandy Cue and Edith Morrera (Brazilian). Sandy had already translated the Gospel of Mark and a portion of the Old Testament. Edith taught school every morning to the Indian children. In the afternoon we worked in the medical clinic. We were excited and exhilarated to be a part of our new ministry team.

The jungle was lush and green. The trees were tall—reaching the heavens. Fresh pineapple, bananas, and papaya were growing everywhere. There was seldom a shortage of food. Regularly, the Indian men would come by our house and either offer meat from a wild boar they had killed or fish that was speared in the river.

Soon after arriving at Palimi-U station, we were given part of a catfish to cook that the Indians had caught and traded to the missionaries. They told us the fish in its entirety was six feet long and could have weighed six hundred pounds!

Seasons were either dry or rainy. The days were very hot and the nights were very cool. Since we lived on the equator it seemed like you could almost reach out and touch the moon. One of the Indians pointed to it one night and said, "That's where you came from, isn't it?" The Indian children were fascinated with our white skin and would often gather around to rub our hands and arms to see what it felt like.

Debbie and I were so confident that the Brazilian government would grant our permanent visas that we decided to have all our possessions that had been packed and stored in crates flown down from the States. We believed this would be our home for the rest of our lives.

CHAPTER 7

Bloodshed

Without the shedding of blood there is no forgiveness of sins.

—Hebrews 9:22

The missionaries in North Amazon had been praying for years that the gospel would break through among the Yanomamo. These tribal people were chained to their past traditions and under the control of the witch doctors. Our villagers lived in constant fear of their enemy villages.

One night Sandy knocked on our door and said she heard that Maita was laying paralyzed in his hammock. I quickly got my flashlight and we made our way to the large village house.

Maita's eyes were glazed and his body was stiff. The witch doctor was blowing ash dust on his face, and chanting. As we knelt beside Maita's seemingly lifeless body, he reluctantly moved out of the way.

Sandy asked me to pray. I petitioned God to show his power and remove the evil spirit. We then left and returned to our homes.

Early the next morning we awoke to see some of the Indians running up to our porch, chanting and raving. One of them was Maita. He was full of life and his face aglow. Oh, how we praised God for delivering him from the evil spirit and for dramatically displaying his power to these dear people.

One day Debbie and Edith visited with one of the women in the village moments after she had given birth to a baby girl. The baby was still wet with blood. The mother was holding her close in her arms.

This was big! In the Yanomamo tradition, it was the custom to let the baby be born and drop to the ground. If someone picked it up then it was to be allowed to live. But, if it was a girl, it could be killed on the spot or allowed to just eventually die on the ground. This day, the mother chose to save the baby.

When Debbie and I packed for Brazil we made sure we included a copy of *The Merck Manual*. It is the most widely used medical resource in the world. It was our Jungle Bible. We could rely on its information to tell us what to do in case of a snake bite or how to deliver a baby. In a similar way, we were depending on God's Word for spiritual survival.

How would we ever connect the gospel to their primitive culture? Missionaries had discovered this tribe twenty years earlier. Up until now, the Indians had shown little interest. They did like to hear the story of Judas. They knew about treachery and deception. And, they told us their ancestors passed down a story about a great flood that once covered the earth.

Then one day, it happened. There was a huge roar coming from upriver. Villagers where Maita had come from were rapidly canoeing down river. As the canoes came closer, the sound grew louder.

In a matter of minutes both tribes were headed to the village house. One of the Indians stopped for a moment at our house and motioned for me to come. I quickly grabbed my camera, and without thinking, ran after him. I guess I thought I was in an Indiana Jones movie.

I managed to sneak in the side entrance and was met with dust flying everywhere. Men from both villages were raising their bows and arrows and machetes high in the air, giving warlike chants. There was chaos everywhere. For a moment I wondered if I had made the right decision to come.

In the middle of the darkness I could make out a circle of people and a fight going on. I took my camera, held it high in that direction and snapped a few pictures, not knowing what would appear.

It turns out that two men, one from each village, had been thrust out into a circle. The two squared off against each other, swapping blows to the other's chest. It was known as the chest pounding duel. In Missouri we called it swapping licks, only here it could result in death. After using their fists, they turned to pounding each other with sharp stones. Then they were given machetes.

This went on for about twenty minutes. I was amazed how quickly the whole ordeal started and how quickly it stopped. When it ended the two bleeding men were heading down to the river to wash their wounds. Others went to their hammocks. Life returned to normal. The disgruntled villagers from upriver slowly reassembled and headed home.

Later on, I had a conversation with fellow missionary Steve Anderson and he explained how these two villages were acting out their judicial system. This was the jungle way to resolve disputes, and the good news was it fit right into the presentation of the gospel!

According to Yanomamo tradition, when something bad occurs in the village, the chief takes the initiative to resolve the situation. In our village dispute, one of our men had gone upriver and stolen a woman and brought her back to be his wife. Villagers had wind of it and raced downriver to fight a chest pounding duel with the Palimi-U villagers.

The custom was for two innocent men to be chosen to fight on behalf of the families and villages involved. The chest is beaten because that's where the badness is. When the chief sees the blood flow, he signals the fight is over and there is reconciliation. Sometimes the fighting goes too far and men die.

Long ago, the Big Chief (God) in the sky looked down on the people of earth and saw badness in the chest of all the people. The Big Chief took the initiative to solve the problem by sending his only Son, who was innocent of any badness, to fight for us.

How long did the fight last? God's Banana Leaf (the Bible) says that just as in their chest pounding duels, blood had to flow. It reads, "Without the shedding of blood there is no forgiveness of sin" (Hebrews 9:22).

In the Indian context the men would most likely have to fight their battle all over again. But Jesus fought our battle one time and we are no longer enemies. This reconciliation lasts forever!

When this truth was introduced to the surrounding jungle villages, the gospel became real for the first time and many decided to follow God's path.

***

Debbie and I first came across the name Cherith during those early days in Brazil. Palimi-U station was named after the river that flowed in front of our house. One day I was reading 1 Kings 17 that told of the prophet Elijah being taken care of at the brook Cherith (*Kerith* in Hebrew). Elijah drank from the brook and ravens fed him there in the morning and evening.

It was a difficult time in Israel. Four hundred and ninety prophets followed Baal and another four hundred and sixty followed Ashteroth. Elijah alone stood for God. He announced to King Ahab that there would be no rain until it was time, which was three and a half years.

Being in danger, God led Elijah to hide east of the Jordan River and provided for him there at the tiny brook. This temporary winter stream only appeared for a season. It was a place of isolation. There was good reason to be afraid. While alone, Elijah had to learn total dependence upon God, before the miracle of the fiery sacrifice on Mt. Carmel could take place.

The name Cherith means *to cut off.* Even though Elijah was cut off from his people, God would provide for him. Debbie and I were reflecting on how we, too, were depending on God while adjusting to the lonely, primitive setting of the jungles of the North Amazon.

Some have asked if there was ever a time when we lived in the jungle that we felt afraid. I'm sure Debbie could speak to some scary moments, like when she had her first flight in a small airplane, enduring the canoe ride at Mucajai, or seeing a large poisonous snake in the yard. But, her fears were more for Destiny and her safety.

I personally don't recall being afraid. At our jungle station the Indians watched out for us. Though the tribal people would often war among other villages, I never really felt our family was in danger.

It seems we had the mindset that when you're doing God's will and serving him there was nothing to fear. We always felt protected by his peace (Philippians 4:6-7). We gained confidence from reading about former missionaries, like John and Betty Stam, who were executed by Chinese Communists in the early 1930s. Their testimony reassured us that even in the worst of circumstances, God is sovereign and can be trusted.

We were stationed in a primitive jungle, thousands of miles away from family and hundreds of miles interior to the nearest road. The only way in was to paddle by canoeing upriver through many rapids or to fly by single engine plane with MAF.

I asked Debbie what she thought about naming our next daughter Cherith and she agreed it was perfectly fitting.

Settling into our new home, we had anticipated that we would be permanent residents in the jungle, developing a church among the Yanomamo. But in time, just like the brook in the Bible, our ministry in Brazil would dry up. It appeared only for a season.

CHAPTER 8

Left Behind

With God, behind every *no* is a bigger *yes*.
—Pastor Robert Alderman

Each evening I would take my bath in the Palimi-U River. It was just a stone's throw from our house. Yes, there were piranhas in the river, but now I was an almost fearless twenty-three-year-old. Debbie preferred a nice warm bath in a fifty-five gallon drum that was cut in half and used as a tub.

I was proud of Debbie. She learned to cook our meals over a wood stove and got used to our kerosene refrigerator. She even had the luxury of an old-fashioned ringer washer and the hot sun for drying laundry!

Each night I would crank up the generator for a few hours to give light to the house. With the walls made of slats, it meant there was easy access for unwanted creatures to enter.

Once there was a bat flying around—no problem. I got the machete, and when he landed between two of the slats, I carefully disposed of him. In order to keep mosquitos, frogs, or critters from sleeping with us, we hung mosquito netting over our bed.

The nights when we did have electricity we'd read books, letters from home, or study. Every Friday night we met with the two single missionaries and played Scrabble while eating banana chips.

Every now and then I'd listen to the Armed Forces radio station to get the news or take in a football game from back in the States. For entertainment, we'd laugh our heads off listening to tapes of comedian Jerry Clower as he told hilarious tales of growing up in Mississippi.

We were surprised to learn that the area we were requesting to live in was in a strategic fly zone, too close to the Brazilian and Venezuelan borders. The government of Brazil was very particular about foreigners living in the area. It was not to be our last surprise.

Incredibly, the day after our house was finished we received a short wave radio message from our mission headquarters in Boa Vista. Our permanent visas had been denied and we had two weeks to leave the country. The little MAF airplane would fly out that afternoon to pick us up.

We were in shock! Things were happening so fast, there wasn't much time to think. We took what belongings we had with us from the station, said hasty goodbyes to our coworkers, and flew out to Boa Vista.

Once there, we opened up all our crates that contained everything we owned. We took out a few irreplaceable items and then nailed them back shut. It would have cost too much to bring it all back to the States.

I called our home church in Virginia and told Pastor Alderman the eventful news. If ever there was a time when we needed encouragement, it was now.

Bob said, "Mike, I want you and Debbie to hold on to this. With God, behind every *no* is a bigger *yes*."

At the airport, the officials stamped these words in our passports: "leaving under the shame of deportation." We learned we were not actually being deported—it was the only stamp the official had at the moment.

While flying back to the United States I kept thinking, *What will we tell our supporting churches?* We had assured them God was calling us to Brazil. As we approached New York City and US soil I remember feeling somewhat disillusioned. Had all this been for nothing?

When we went through customs in New York, the agent took one look at the deportation stamp in our passports, smiled and said, "Looks like you won't be going anywhere for a long time."

In departing Brazil, except for a few suitcases, Debbie and I left everything behind. What good could possibly come out of all this?

***

Upon our return to the States we were invited to serve at one of our supporting churches for a year, while determining where God was leading us next. I was asked to be the worship and youth leader at Pleasant Ridge Baptist Church in Ellisville, Mississippi, where Reverend Herschel Bragg was the senior pastor.

We began our ministry there in February, 1980. Laurel was the nearby city where Cherith Dawn McCrum entered the world on May 30th. It also was the city where Walt and Valerie Shepard had moved to pastor a church. Valerie was the only child of Jim and Elisabeth Elliot.

I got to meet Elisabeth when I visited her daughter and family during a book signing. She signed an original copy of *Life* magazine that my mom had given me. It reported the story of Jim's death back in 1956. I remember her saying, "Well, *that's* an antique!"

We dove into ministry and spent a lot of time discipling the youth. Tim Weems, one of twenty students in the youth group, is now a pastor of a nearby church in Mississippi.

While in Brazil I met some missionary men who had gone to Dallas Theological Seminary (DTS). I marveled at how well and how clearly they taught the Scriptures, making the Bible come alive.

The experience at PRBC verified that God was preparing me to be a pastor, but I also realized I needed more Bible and pastoral training. God soon opened the door to attend DTS, a prestigious institution with a historical legacy through its founder Lewis Sperry Chafer. We resigned the church in May of 1981, and left for Dallas, Texas.

Even though the timing was right, it would take us a lot of faith to make the move. I was barely a C student in college. But, DTS agreed to accept me based on my ministry experience and put me on probation for the first semester. No problem. I was able to have a great academic semester and the probation was lifted.

I remember how hot that first summer was in Dallas. For over thirty days it never got below 100 degrees during the day and ninety at night. We found a house to rent in Mesquite, a southeastern suburb of Dallas and I secured a great part-time job making $16 an hour (substantial wages at the time) at Gordon's Transports, a freight company on the northern side of Dallas. We were so excited to be entering this new phase of our ministry life.

Living in Dallas and going to seminary was a highlight in our young married life. Eventually, we had two more children. Amber Deane McCrum was born on July 28, 1982, in Mesquite Hospital and Robert "Robby" Duane McCrum was born on September 7, 1984, at Baylor Medical Center in Dallas. Through God's provision, we had insurance with the seminary that paid for each birth and the hospital fees—around $1,000 each.

We became members at Mesquite Valley Baptist Church and sat under the great teaching ministry of Dr. Floyd Elmore. He and his wife Pam would become a tremendous encouragement to Debbie and me during our seminary days.

In September, I registered for school, signed up for my fall classes and took out a school loan of $275 a month for that first year. We had things planned so that we would make it financially.

I was thrilled that I would actually be having classes taught by some incredible professors and authors. Dr. Howard Hendricks and Dr. Roy Zuck would teach *Bible Study Methods*. I also would get to study under the likes of Dr. John Walvoord, Dr. Dwight Pentecost, Dr. Norm Geisler, Dr. Charles Ryric, and Dr. Stanley Touissaint. Dr. Touissaint became my favorite professor.

I came home after that first day of classes and called into work. Unfortunately, my supervisor told me I had been laid off. We couldn't believe it! I remember thinking, *God I thought you had called us to go to seminary?*

I immediately began a new search for employment. There were openings at UPS, but I felt it would be too stressful to work there and do school at the same time. I did some furniture moving jobs, but they didn't pay much.

After a few weeks we noticed an ad in the classified section of a Dallas newspaper looking to hire a custom picture framer at Rhodes Gallery. I called, told them about my situation and about my framing experience in college. Mrs. Betty Rhodes invited me to come for an interview and she hired me on the spot. She was a Godsend.

The only downside was that I would be working twice the hours that I worked for Gordon, for half the salary. We could still pay our monthly bills except for the school loan. Where would we find an extra $275 per month?

One day we received a letter in the mail. It was from the missionaries we worked with in Brazil. They asked if they could sell the items we had left behind to the other missionaries at a yard sale of sorts. They would set a fair price and send us the money from the sale. We thought it was a nice gesture, but really didn't think much would come from it, so we agreed.

To our surprise for the next year we received a check in the mail every month for no less than $275. God used the items we left behind in Brazil to pay for my first year's school bill!

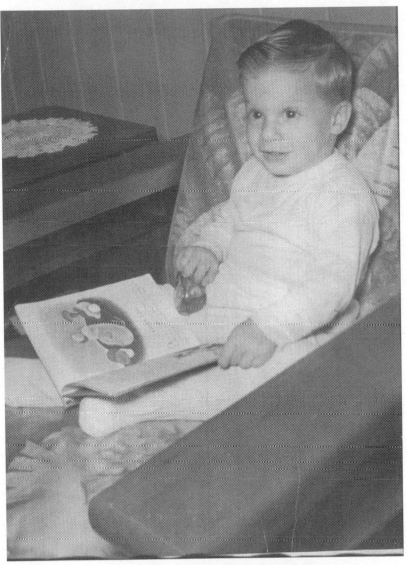

Mike with his favorite bedtime
book, *Chicken Little.*

Duane McCrum family in
August, 1964: Duane and Jean,
Larry, Roger, Mike, Sharon.

John and Thelma McCrum at
their 50th wedding anniversary
celebration in July, 1969.

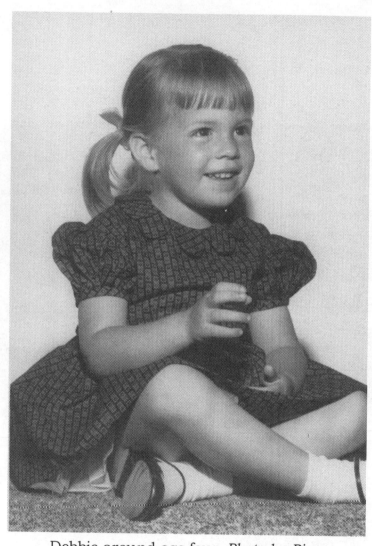

Debbie around age four. *Photo by Pixy Pin-Ups with Dunbar-Stanley Studios, NC*

Hubert Ferrell family in July, 1978. Back
row: Patti, Becky, Debbie, Peggy, Melissa.
Front row: Susie, Olive and Hubert.

Our wedding day, August 15,
1975. *Photo by Alton Davis*

Morning of our first flight into
the jungle April, 1979.

Palimi-U station, Roraíma, Brazil. Our
home for five months. Clockwise from
left, grass airstrip, mission compound,
Indian village house, Palimi-U River.

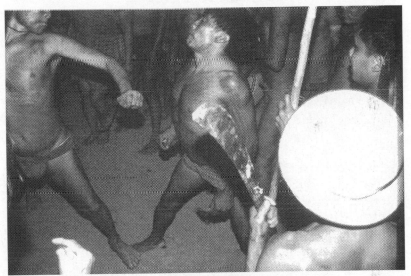

Chest pounding duel. The Yanomamo
way of settling disputes between
villages often led to death.

CHAPTER 9

Blind Man

I don't know what happened to my husband,
but I want whatever he's got!

—Maura Reyna

During my high school years in Missouri my eye doctor discovered some irregularities in both my corneas. I remember him asking me if I was on drugs. The corneas were warping and becoming cone shaped. That's when we discovered I had *Keratoconus*, a degenerative eye disease. The doctor told me that one day I would need corneal transplants.

My rigorous study regimen at DTS seemed to accelerate the condition and make it worse. It progressed to the point that I couldn't wear contact lenses without pain. I was extremely sensitive to light. I even had to wear two pairs of sunglasses and peek through my fingers while driving to and from campus.

We were committed to God's call on our life. He always had been faithful before. He had supplied for my first year of school—certainly he could provide for us now—and he did. God raised up a part-time youth and worship ministry position at our church, under Floyd's leadership.

As the pain in my eyes grew worse, my dream of being a pastor seemed to fade. After all, who would want a blind pastor? When I couldn't take the pain anymore my eye doctor agreed that it was time for transplants on both eyes.

In 1983 this was a relatively new procedure. At the time, the best US hospital to have the surgery was at Presbyterian Hospital in Dallas, Texas. I was in the right place at the right time.

As students we didn't have money for the surgeries, so Floyd encouraged me to contact the seminary for financial assistance. By the Lord's provision again, DTS paid for all of my surgery and medical bills for the transplant on my left eye. It was around $4,000.

In turn, the school asked if they could send out a fund-raising letter to alumni with our story. The response was the largest amount of financial gifts ever received in its history.

The first surgery took place in December of 1983. Christmas was especially joyful that year. Soon after I went in to the hospital, a donor with the right blood type was found.

The first corneal tissue came from a forty-nine year-old woman who died of a heart attack and the second from a thirty-seven year-old man killed in a car accident. We were so thankful for these two dear folks who had selflessly been part of an organ donor program. Debbie mused, "Since you now have a woman's cornea, you'll be able to see things from a woman's perspective!"

My eye healed quickly. Within a few weeks my vision had improved dramatically and I could see 20/20 with corrective lenses. The pain and light sensitivity were gone.

The next year I had the transplant performed on my right eye, with that surgery costing $6,000. The seminary, along with my brother Roger's church in South Africa, helped meet the need. In addition, to paying for the surgeries, DTS also gave me a tuition grant in order to continue my classwork in the spring term.

The second surgery and healing process turned out to be a little more complicated. This time stitches had to come out to shape the cornea. Unfortunately, they were embedded and had to be dug out.

I was to be awake during the entire procedure. The doctor said, "My instruments are very sharp. Whatever you do, don't blink. I could cut your eyelid in two."

I remembered something my mom would do when she went to the dentist. She would focus on Christ and the cross. I tried it, and it worked!

These surgeries enabled me to continue and finish my studies. It wasn't easy, but with Debbie's encouragement, I endured. We were constantly being reminded of God's faithfulness to our family.

However, the eye disease, long hours at work, and my focus on studies began to take a toll on our family. One day Destiny asked, "Mom, when is Daddy ever going to finish school?"

***

In April, 1983, Floyd accepted a teaching position at Cedarville College in Ohio. He recommended to the congregation that I become the new pastor and I received a unanimous vote.

At Mesquite Valley Baptist Church, I wanted to train our people how to share the gospel. The approach we used was taught by Ed Scearce called *Evangelism Explosion* (EE). We memorized Scripture, learned how to initiate conversation, how to ask the right questions, and practice it one-on-one with each other.

DEBBIE: *On February 16, 1985, I was practicing my gospel presentation for the Evangelism Explosion class. Six-and-a-half-year-old Destiny was listening to me ask the questions. The first one was "Have you come to the place in your spiritual life where you know for certain that if you were to die, you'd go to heaven?"*

Destiny interrupted me twice. "Mom, I don't know for certain."

I replied, "Shh, I'm trying to practice."

I asked question number two: "Now, if you were to die and stand before God and he said 'Why should I let you into my heaven?' What would you say?"

Destiny blurted out again, "Mom, I have reached the point in my spiritual life where I want to know I'm going to heaven!" I was surprised and elated. Mike and I both took time to pray with her and she placed her trust in Christ.

I was given a list of those who recently moved into our community and took a team to visit the John Reyna family. When we arrived at the house, I saw a man under his car, apparently changing his oil. I said, "John Reyna?" He was startled and bumped his head on the engine. (He told me later that he was afraid that I was the police looking for him.)

I asked if we could visit for a few minutes. We introduced ourselves and told him why we had come. John listened to the gospel presentation. He said he had never heard the gospel explained quite like this and blurted out that he wanted to have the assurance of his salvation. We knelt beside his couch and John prayed to receive Christ.

He then told us his wife Maura was kicking him out of the house. He asked if we'd come back next week to tell her what we told him. He thought he could persuade her to delay his departure one more week.

When we returned, before we could ring the doorbell, Maura opened the door and invited us in. When we sat down on the couch she immediately turned to me and said, "I don't know what happened to my husband. But, I want whatever he's got!" That night we knelt together and Maura followed in the steps of her husband. A few weeks later we had the privilege of celebrating with them in baptism.

Jesus was on his way to Jerusalem when he encountered a blind man begging by the side of the road (Luke 18:35-43). When he asked the man what he wanted the man said, "I want to see!" That day the Great Physician not only healed him physically, but he also gave him spiritual sight.

***

In the fall of 1983 my grandmother Thelma McCrum died and we drove back to Missouri for her funeral. My cousins, Dave and Pat Warren, came from Ohio to attend, as well. Dave had graduated from Dallas Theological Seminary and was now a professor at Cedarville College. He had been very close to my dad before his death.

After the service he asked me how things were going with my eyes. I told him how it had been a real struggle, but that I hoped to graduate on time. He then spoke about a conversation he had with my dad years before.

It seems my mom and dad had developed a deep interest in the Warrens, so much so that they wanted to attend his DTS graduation. My parents drove from Missionary Acres to Dallas and on the way the transmission in their car went out. They had to take a train the rest of the way to get to Dave's graduation in time.

At my grandmother's funeral Dave related that my dad told him how envious he was of him studying at DTS. In his words, "I'd give my right arm to be able to go to Dallas Seminary." Dave told me my dad would be proud of me. That was all I needed to go back and finish strong, and I did.

My mom wasn't able to attend my graduation. She needed to stay back to attend my sister Sharon's graduation at Tennessee Temple College. So, it meant a lot to see my brother Roger and his wife, Darlene, make the trip to Dallas.

Dave and Pat and two of their kids drove all the way from Ohio to be there. I couldn't believe it! He told me they did it because my dad had come to theirs. And, the transmission in their car went out, as well!

The graduation ceremonies were very special to me. Andy Stanley (now Senior Pastor at North Point Community Church in Alpharetta, Georgia) was in our class and his father, Dr. Charles Stanley (Senior Pastor at First Baptist Church Atlanta), spoke at the baccalaureate service.

At graduation we arrived at the auditorium a little early and were able to meet and get a picture with one of the seminary board members: Tom Landry, former coach of the Dallas Cowboys.

On May 5, 1985, I graduated with my Masters in Biblical Studies. I couldn't have made it without Debbie's support. The same day she earned her very coveted Pht (Pushing Hubby Through) degree.

CHAPTER 10

No Mistake

Mommy, are you EVER going to let me ask
Jesus into my heart?

—Amber

One of my greatest joys during seminary was serving
as pastor at Mesquite Valley. The church was small
in size but large in love. The ten families we served
will always remain dear to our hearts. We knew our
time with them was for a short season.

After graduation we felt the need to move closer
to both our parents. My mom was a widow and
Debbie's dad's cancer had returned. I signed up on
a placement board at DTS seeking a new ministry
position in the Southeast.

In October, 1985, I received a phone call from
Gene Schrader, an elder at Fellowship Bible Church
in Roswell, Georgia. My resume was the last of fifty
the elders were reviewing. He invited us to interview
for the youth pastor position.

Dan DeHaan, Joe Usry, Lee Eskew, Charlie Lindsey, Charlie Morgan, Bob White, and Norm Smith had met weekly for two years in a Roswell office to pray for God to raise up a non-denominational church in North Metro Atlanta. These men wanted to be a part of a church that would focus on three values: (1) teaching the Scriptures, (2) discipling men, and (3) living out the example of Acts 2:42, where the body of believers minister to one another.

God answered their prayer and in September, 1979, a group of sixty people signed the original charter. On Sunday, October 7th, the group had their first worship service as a church at Mimosa Elementary School with one hundred and twenty in attendance. Joe Usry, Art Vander Veen, Bob Roland, and Myles Lorenzen were soon hired as pastors.

Within a year the church multiplied and established three more FBC-like churches in nearby counties. By the time we arrived, FBC Roswell had grown to eight hundred members, using the Roswell Roller Rink and adjacent fitness center for worship and fellowship groups.

***

We drove from Dallas to Atlanta with four young children for a weekend interview. When we arrived I went in to the church office to meet Gene. He came down the stairs and looked at me kind of funny. I guess we must have looked a little tired and disheveled. I didn't think much of it—we were so excited to be there. We were just as excited to learn that we would be staying with a lovely couple, Ken and Phyllis Ott, our hosts for the weekend.

Saturday was eventful. During the day I was able to spend some quality time with the youth on a community service project. That evening we were scheduled to have dinner with Gene and the Youth Leadership Team at the home of David and Jane Williams. This was a group of about twelve parents, including a few elders, who made up the search committee. The meal and conversation were fantastic. We thought things were going surprisingly well.

What we didn't know was that Gene had called the group to come a half-hour early to discuss our candidacy. We learned later that he had told them how sorry he was for inviting us to interview.

"We made a mistake," he said.

He told them, in fairness, after dinner he would let us share a little about ourselves and then say goodbye.

After the meal we all gathered in the living room. Gene asked us to tell our story and why we wanted to come to FBC. I went first and shared that I was born in Hawaii to missionary parents and that I grew up in Missouri, where I trusted Christ as my Savior at the age of seven.

I related the story of my dad's death and how that event set the course of direction for my life. I told how God used this experience to help me understand and relate to parents and their children, especially when they were going through tough times.

That's when the mood of the room changed. I noticed tears on some of the faces. Debbie followed, and afterwards the questions began to come. Wow, we felt so wanted. One parent even commented that the church was going through some challenges with their youth and families, and they thought the two of us could be a great help.

It wasn't until months later that we learned what happened that Saturday night after Debbie and I left the meeting to return to our host home.

It seems that Gene had signaled to the team to stay behind to discuss the McCrums. He told the group he was sorry for trying to close the book on us and confessed to the team, "We would have made a bigger mistake had we not chosen Mike and Debbie to come."

On December 10th, the Youth Leadership team notified us of their unanimous decision for me to serve as youth pastor.

In January, Gene preached one Sunday morning on "Faith." His text was 2 Corinthians 5:7, which reads: "For we walk by faith, not by sight." In his sermon he disclosed the story about what happened during the interview process. He recounted how at first he had gone by sight, not by faith. When we came to candidate, I did not come across as the typical charismatic youth pastor.

He went on to explain how the hearts and minds of the youth and parent leadership team were changed after hearing our testimonies and seeing our passion to serve youth and their families.

Then, Gene tearfully affirmed us before the congregation and announced that I'd be joining the staff team on February 1st. Norm Smith, a local realtor, helped us find a house, and we were able to move into our Woodstock home the day before my start date.

We didn't know a church like FBC existed. It was the perfect place to serve the Lord and raise a family. The church families had the same values we had for our children. And, when Debbie's father died of lung cancer on April 30, 1986, it sure was good to have the love and support of our new church family.

I can't say enough about men like Roy Ludwig, Gayle Jackson, Chuck Harley, Gene Schrader, Charlie Lindsey, Lew Miller, David Williams, Jim Lott, and Bill Regehr who built into my life those early years and helped me become a leader. God was faithful to surround me with godly men, who modeled Christ and helped me grow spiritually.

***

DEBBIE: *On May 2, 1988, our seven-and-one-half-year-old Cherith showed interest in trusting in Christ as her Savior. While I was tucking her into bed and praying for her, she asked if she could ask Jesus into her heart.*

Before I could answer her, Amber responded, "Me, too! Me, too!" I sent Cherith to Mike so he could pray with her and told Amber (with a hug) that it was not a "me, too" event and that she could ask Jesus into her heart someday. I wasn't sure that at five years of age she was ready for such a big step.

I continued to pray for Amber and several months later on October 16, 1988, at the age of six, she asked me at bedtime, "Mommy, are you EVER going to let me ask Jesus into my heart?" I chuckled, gave her a hug, and sent her downstairs to Daddy's lap for some chatting and praying.

Robby also showed great interest in Jesus from an early age. When he was four years old we were driving everyone home from school when we encountered a tornado. The sky turned green, the winds blew fiercely, and the rain pounded. I was trying to get us to a friend's house for safety and I shushed the children so I could concentrate.

Breaking through the silence, from the back seat came Robby's little voice singing, "God is my helper; he takes care of me. He's right beside me, loving constantly. When I need God's help, I know that I can pray..." It was a song he had sung in Learning Center at church and knew it was for when you're afraid. We felt better as he sang and made it safely to Tricia Blumberg's home to wait out the storm.

On September 10, 1991, a few days after Robby turned seven, he had been riding his bicycle in the cul-de-sac. He came inside a bit later and found me. "Mom," he said. "I wanted to tell you something, but I needed to pop a few more wheelies, and then I told myself I'd come and tell you."

By now, I was quite curious, not just because of what he said, but for the serious expression on his little face. "I'm ready to ask Jesus into my heart right now!" he said. I was so happy, and I told him that Dad would be home soon and we'd all sit down and have a chat.

Mike and I had prayed for our children's salvation from the time they were born. We determined that *they would be taught the way of salvation, but that we'd allow them to let us know when they were ready to begin their own journey of faith.*

***

Our children were a part of the first school year of Fellowship Christian Academy. God was faithful. The staff families were given a discount on the tuition. We would never have been able to afford a private Christian school of this caliber.

At FCA our kids received a quality education that included sports and other extra-curricular activities. We're so thankful for Dave Kinsey, one of the headmasters who helped develop FCA into the wonderful school it is today.

We also were so blessed to have been a part of a church that had an incredible Children's Ministry, led by Corinne Simpson and Sherilyn Leath. The same was true of the Youth Ministry, led by Mike Baumgardner and Jim Moon. Our four kids were taught the Scriptures, discipled in small groups, and nurtured by these quality folks. The camps and houseboat retreats were memorable, life-changing events.

The church held its annual picnic and baptism at a youth camp by the Chattahoochee River. I was privileged to baptize Destiny and Amber in the swimming pool one special Sunday afternoon.

When each of the girls turned twelve years old, we dressed up and went on a formal date to a restaurant. I read them a letter I had written and gave them a purity ring. Here's a portion of what I wrote:

> As your father, I want you to know that I love you very much and that I want to be there beside you to encourage you during these special days of youth. You're a very beautiful young lady and many guys will try to come around to try and steal your heart. My prayer is that you'll remain pure and not give your heart to another man until you feel he is worthy to have it and you're ready to marry.
>
> Because you're so valuable to me I want to initiate a covenant between me and you that will last until your wedding day. I want you to prepare yourself for your husband by keeping yourself free from sexual involvement until marriage. I'm giving you a gold ring for you to wear as a continual reminder of our commitment and trust to each other. It's to be worn up to your wedding day and presented to your husband during the wedding ceremony.

Robby's ceremony came in the form of a manhood trip down the Nantahala River. We went fishing, set up camp, and cooked our dinner. Around the campfire I read him letters from me and some men who wanted to speak into his life.

As a family, we found many ways to have fun together. The girls and I constructed a playhouse and Robby and I built an eighteen-foot high castle, complete with a draw bridge and tower.

We thought it was important to make every effort to attend our kids' church and school activities, special programs, and sporting events. When Destiny was in junior high she wrote me the following letter:

> Every basketball game that I played in seventh and eighth grade you were there. It didn't matter that I never scored more than two points or that I never started, you were always there. When I played I played for you. I will never forget when I made my very first two points. I came running down the court yelling "I did it! I did it!" You jumped to your feet and yelled to everyone around you, "That's my girl! That's my girl!" That day will always stick in my mind!

Our friend, Lee Eskew, would ride along with me to Destiny's high school basketball games. Her senior year at Sequoyah her team won the state championship.

Robby played baseball and soccer, but his greatest joy was to work on cars. He loved to take the engines apart and try to put them back together. Today, he knows everything mechanical about trucks and automobiles.

Debbie and I knew it was important for our kids to "always be ready to give a defense to everyone who asks you a reason for the hope that is in you" (1 Peter 3:15). We taught them from an early age to share their faith.

Through an FBC friend, Geoff Wiggins, Amber learned how to share her faith with people of other faiths. The opportunity came one day when her high school class was having lunch at a Mexican restaurant. She was sharing with her Mormon friend why she was glad to be a follower of Jesus. One of the reasons that she shared was, "because I know that I am going to heaven when I die."

Another classmate was listening in on the conversation and told Amber later that she wanted to have that assurance. She had been having trouble sleeping at night because her brother's friend had recently been killed in a tragic bicycle accident, while training for the Olympics. Amber lovingly showed her from the Bible how she could know she was going to heaven.

Turns out, each night as she was falling asleep, the young lady had asked God, "If you are real, would you send someone to tell me about you?" When Amber recounted the story, we were awed by God's faithfulness!

***

Our kids had a hard time dealing with what had happened to their sister Cherith. They were all very close to her, especially Amber. She couldn't wait for her to return from the cruise to let her be the first one to know she was pregnant with her second child.

I thought I could help, so I asked her to lunch and shared from my story how God allows sorrow and suffering for his glory and our good. I told her that my dad's death was not a mistake and if he had not been killed, they most likely would not have hired me to be the youth pastor at FBC.

I said, "Amber, I know you're very sad. I'm very sad, too. I don't know all that God has planned ahead for us, but one thing is for certain. What happened to Cherith was no mistake."

CHAPTER 11

Mission:937

The harvest is plentiful, but the workers are few. Pray earnestly to the Lord of the harvest to send out laborers into his harvest.

—Matthew 9:37-38

In our first year at Fellowship I found specialists at Emory Hospital in Atlanta to handle my eye condition. I was placed under the care of Dr. George Waring and Mr. Buddy Russell.

In 2005, I would have another cornea transplant on my left eye performed by the leading eye surgeon in the Southeast, Dr. Doyle Stulting. I'm deeply grateful to these men, especially Buddy. He was able to fit me with special scleral contact lenses so that I could see without pain.

Also, in that first year at FBC I was asked to develop and lead the world missions program. The ministry had built a good foundation under the leadership of Myles Lorenzen and Gary Klingler. A couple of youth had been on a Teen Missions trip and the church's first short-term mission trip had been taken to Haiti.

During our first summer at FBC we took the youth to downtown Atlanta to serve a church in a difficult area. Bob Lupton, Director of Family Consultation Services near Grant Park, helped arrange the opportunity. The Ricky Dill Family organized the week's events. We provided a VBS for the children in the neighborhood, and slept on the pews of the church. We were thankful we were able to be an encouragement to the youth minister.

Our first world missions conference was held in the fall of 1988. We invited national pastors and church planters who were impacting nations to be a part of the week-long celebration. Joseph and Esther Tan from Singapore, David and Helen Kelawing from East Malaysia, Birbal and Annette Boodram, and Siddhant and Beulah Yogi from Trinidad, were a special part of that first conference.

Elisabeth Elliot spoke to the Women's Ministry. Graham Sumner flew over from England to help us plan short-term mission trips. The guest missionaries stayed in the homes of families in our congregation. We thought it was important to always make sure there was time in the week's schedule to honor them and build into their lives.

The world missions conference found its permanent place on the calendar in February and was one of the highlights of the church year. We brought in our missionaries from around the world to share their ministry vision and report on how the Lord was blessing. Keynote speakers, such as Paul Smith, Al Larson, Ramesh Richard, Ron Blue, and J. Robertson McQuilkin, yearly challenged our church to become "senders" of the gospel.

An important feature of the week's events was for our families to host missionaries in a home group setting. We always hosted a group and encouraged our kids to participate. These life-changing moments gave Destiny, Cherith, Amber, and Robby a heart for world missions.

During conference week the missionaries would stay in member's homes and be treated to special, elaborate dinners. I'm grateful for Judy Regehr, my Administrative Assistant, who coordinated everyone's schedule and kept multiple events flowing smoothly. She was incredible!

About a hundred FBCers went on short-term trips each summer. We loved taking our kids with us to Robbinsville, North Carolina to serve the Cherokee Indians. Our hosts were Mack and Shirley Oswalt who were leaders in the Snowbird community. Shirley is a Native American and part of the Eastern Band of the Cherokee Nation. This annual weeklong event ended up being our family's missions ministry for ten consecutive years.

Families camped out in tents beside Little Snowbird Baptist Church. The tents were grouped in clusters and we named them after Atlanta suburbs. We had Buckhead with its flower pots and rocking chairs on the "porch" of the tent. And then there was our tent. It was in the "Cherokee County" area—probably because when it rained the roof leaked.

We conducted VBS for the Indian children and adult teams worked on needy projects in the community. Each summer we baptized people in the cold mountain stream. I baptized Eddie Tuck, one of our faithful team members, at a spot called Elijah's Pool.

There were morning chapel times that set the spiritual tone for the day's activities. Sitting around a large campfire was the perfect ending to a full day. Some of our dearest friendships were developed on those trips.

Al Hanson, George Deuel, and Bill Tuck became the team leaders and led several mission trips to Robbinsville. A few years into the ministry, Mike and Marsha Harwood were called by the Lord to move to Snowbird and serve as full-time missionaries. They have a thriving ministry in the community to this day.

We named the missions program Mission:937, based on Jesus' admonition in Matthew 9:37-38: "The harvest is plentiful, but the workers are few. Pray the Lord of the harvest to send forth laborers into his harvest."

Our ministry core was made up of David and Jane Williams, Chris and Terri Browne, Doc and Mindy Parrish, Donna Smith, and George and Barbara Deuel. These men and their wives established a successful missions ministry that impacted the world. They gave me the nickname "Bwana." The word means *Leader* in Swahili.

A summer team to Trinidad served as a real encouragement to the Yogis and Boodrams, who ministered among Hindu people. Team member Leo Wells and I spent an eventful afternoon with the Yogis. They opened up and shared their struggles with us. They later told us that our time together reassured them, giving them the grace to continue.

Graham, a builder by trade, became an integral part of our summer program, helping us lead teams to Trinidad, Haiti, Singapore, East Malaysia, and Romania. We saw him as a modern-day Apostle Paul. Every trip with him was an adventure, both physically and spiritually. We joking called him Pharaoh, because he "cracked the whip" with the mission work teams.

Our medical mission team was invited to go into Romania after the overthrow of communism on December 25, 1989. With the country still in turmoil, we made contact with doctors in Tigre Neamt and were able to bring in badly needed medical supplies.

A school teacher by the name of Gabriella invited the team to come and speak in English to her class. Graham gave his testimony, and as a result, Gabriella trusted Christ as her Savior. Several others also came to Christ on that trip, and the team was invited to come back the following year.

I was able to be a part of the second team. I couldn't believe my eyes as we crossed the border from Austria into Cluj. It was like going back one hundred years in time. There were ox carts, dreary farm lands, and broken down houses. In the towns, you could still see bullet holes in the walls of buildings. We crossed over the Carpathian Mountains, where Dracula's Castle is located.

The Romanians were so very grateful for our visit and the supplies we brought them. Most of the funds were raised by FBC. Following teams were able to go back and establish and build a church. There are teams of FBCers who still go every summer to help with the orphanages.

Gabriella was able to travel to one of our world missions conferences and got to see America for the first time. I remember her first impressions when she was taken to a supermarket. She marveled at all the food available on the shelves.

We were saddened to learn when she returned to Romania that she went to be with the Lord after suffering an aneurysm. But, God was faithful and many have come to know Christ as a result of her courage and testimony.

Not only were our children able to participate in the Snowbird trips, but during high school, Destiny and Amber each served a month in Ghana, Africa. Destiny also served in Brazil and Mexico, while Amber worked in Guatemala and Trinidad. Cherith and Robby had the opportunity to minister to the poor in the Appalachian Mountain community of West Virginia.

Going on these trips and serving less fortunate people gave them a different perspective on the world. It also taught them to depend on God to supply the finances for each trip. They were encouraged to see him always come through.

I traveled on two mission trips to Sarawak, East Malaysia, with Graham and Joseph Tan. We were joined by an amazing medical team: Dr. Bob Albee, Dr. Dan Hodges, Dr. Craig Smith, Dr. David Williams, and nurses Marye McKinney and Pam Daniell.

We traveled by longboat up the Baram River, and in one day alone, ventured through eighty rapids. Once we reached a village, we provided medical and dental clinics during the day and held church services in the evening.

On one trip we were making our way upriver to the next village when dusk suddenly came upon us. We hit a big wave and our boat filled with water. We were bailing water as fast as we could while maneuvering over to the shore. After a scary few minutes, we found a calm place up against the bank, still bailing water as fast as we could.

Then, while we sat in the boat in stunned silence, Graham started to lead us in the hymn *It is Well with My Soul*. It had a calming effect after the fear-filled experience of nearly capsizing in the rapids. Had we gone over, it would have meant the loss of all our belongings and supplies, and potential drowning.

Eventually, in the darkness we were able to make it to an abandoned village and spend a long night in a bug-infested hut.

Another trip led us to the headwaters of the river. From there we began a two day trek over two mountains to get to the primitive Penan tribe. The climbing was difficult and the heat and humidity wore on us. Stopping along the way, and sitting on a log with teenager John Freeman, I said, "John, I sure hope people back at Fellowship are praying for us. I don't think I can make it."

In a few minutes we felt our strength return and the team was able to make it the rest of the way to the village, where we held a clinic and shared the gospel.

I was too weak to attend the church service and wondered if I had the strength to make the return trip. I remembered when I packed for the trip Debbie had thrown a Snicker's candy bar in my suitcase saying, "You never know." I came across the candy bar and put it in my backpack for the trek back, hoping it would bring me enough energy to make it over the mountains. The next day we started out and returned to base camp with minimal trouble. That candy bar made the difference!

CHAPTER 12

Identity Crisis

I see a beautiful form trapped inside.
—Michelangelo

In 1993 my friend, Roger Dean, sponsored me to go on a men's Tres Dias (three day) retreat in North Georgia. I really didn't want to go. After all, weren't all men's retreats the same?

The truth is I felt stuck. No, it was worse than that. I was the dead skunk in the middle of the road. I was being hunted by hounds in my past and smashed by unmet expectations in the present. Debbie encouraged me to go, hoping that I might regain my desire to move forward.

I found myself living out of the rubbish of adolescent pain. I developed what Greg Miller refers to as "stinking thinking."[13] This mindset occurs when you feel worthless, and then end up believing it. Soon you become controlled by it. This was one of the reasons I battled with self-confidence as a pastor and always feeling like I couldn't measure up.

On that weekend something happened, something almost too wonderful to explain. I was ambushed by God. The Father had been waiting for me, and he captured me with the fire of his love. For three days the Spirit spoke into my life and I came to a deeper realization of the tremendous gift I have received from Christ—grace!

I arrived as a broken, discouraged pastor. Why? I had been defining myself by how I performed in ministry. For years I had been stunted in my spiritual growth because I lived according to my failures. I was crippled by regret, always being followed by my childhood shadow.

I left that weekend with a real, authentic relationship with God. The work the Father did in my life those three days set me free to be the son (his), husband, father, and pastor he intended me to be. He used Tres Dias as a significant tool to reveal my true identity.

An artist in Florence, Italy, once asked the great Renaissance sculptor Michelangelo what he saw when he approached a huge block of marble. "I see a beautiful form trapped inside," he replied, "and it is simply my responsibility to take my mallet and chisel and chip away until the figure is set free."[14]

I came to realize that my heavenly Father had been at work, purposefully drawing me to himself, so that I could experience the fullness of his grace. The awareness of that grace would change me and enable me to become an instrument of grace in the lives of others.

A verse of Scripture that chiseled away at my identity is found in Galatians 4:6: "Because you are sons, God has sent the Spirit of his Son into our hearts, crying, 'Abba! Father!'" The evidence was clear. The Father wanted me to enjoy a personal, intimate relationship with him. I had every reason and right to call him "Daddy."

The image broke through when I was reminded of what Jesus said in John 14:18: "I will not leave you as orphans; I will come to you." His purpose was to "make known the Father's love in me," so that I'd no longer think or act as a slave, but agree that I was a son, an heir with him (John 17:26)!

I reconnected with the reality that the Holy Spirit lives in me. I had someone supernatural to help me walk the journey to the King (John 14:16, 26). I embraced the truth that he manifests the life of Christ in and through me (Galatians 5:17). The more I surrender to the Spirit, he will empower me to be and to do all the Father desires.

With a new identity came a new motivation for living. I now find my source of strength from what Christ did for me on the cross. Galatians 2:20 describes it this way: "I have been crucified with Christ. It is no longer I who live, but Christ who lives in me. And the life I now live in the flesh I live by faith in the Son of God, who loved me and gave himself for me." Following Christ is a matter of life... and death.

During the past twenty years, I've served as a Spiritual Director on over fifty weekend retreats in North and Northeast Georgia, Tallahassee and Tampa, Florida, and in Brussels, Belgium. These communities have experienced many Red Letter Days together. I am forever indebted to the many hundreds of friendships I've developed with men and women through Cursillo, Tres Dias, and Walk to Emmaus.

Some of the men leaders who impacted me most in the early years include Ralph Drew, Don Stewart, Don Munn, Frank Lewis, Bill Furr, Bruce Deel, and Tom Grady. In recent years God has used Bernie McClure, Bundy Sanders, Richard Curran, Dennis Malone, George Flurry, Jimmy Snead, Mick McLaughlin, Bud Leonard, and Lou Harris to help me grow deeper.

Women leaders became an important part of my journey as well—Cheri Furr, Lori McClure, Miriam Dolson, Susan Wing, Michelle Sanders, Anita Rudzinski, Chris Weaver, and Terri Smith, to name a few. I want to give a special word of thanks to *all* the ladies who have allowed me to speak words of encouragement to them on women's weekend retreats.

It would be impossible to name everyone who has helped me grow in grace and teach me to live out the life of Christ in me. You know who you are. Please accept my deepest gratitude.

***

How would I ever move past the events surrounding my father's death? I had disappointed my dad and deeply hurt people I loved. God, and others, had forgiven me, why couldn't I forgive myself? *Because of what you've done* had put up a good fight with my true identity in Christ.

I had given way to a spiraling, debilitating self-condemnation. Over time, my sin and shame continued to enslave me, taking up residence in the cellar of my heart. At the same time God had been at work to free me from my past—to give me a new name. Instead of *Failure*, he wanted my name to be *Forgiven*.

Sometimes, I would imagine myself going over to the cellar door and walking downstairs in the darkness to seek forgiveness from those I'd hurt. But I was too afraid—afraid of opening doors that would unleash more pain. What I didn't realize is the quickest way to heal the soul is through the wounds.

In September 1993, I was finally able to take a giant step forward and grow up in Christ. Ever since Dad died, my brother Roger took interest in me and stepped in to encourage me in the journey. He wrote me a letter from South Africa where he is a missionary. His words were brief, but powerful:

> Yesterday was the anniversary of Dad's death, twenty-four years ago. I've often thought how that we boys had been a disappointment to our father and how he was often ashamed of us. Well, the grace of God does change things Mike. Dad would be very proud of you today, to see how you have faithfully served the Lord in different

capacities. What a joy it will be to share with him in heaven of God's blessings in our lives.

By the time I got to the fourth sentence, I lost it. The emotions had been mired behind a huge dam in my heart. Like a giant tsunami, grace broke through, and the years of struggle gave way. I cried tears of truth that were buried so deep. I saw my father's face. He *did* love me.

I had agonized over how I treated my younger sister after my dad's accident. Sharon was attentive to my struggle and wrote me a letter saying, "I am very sorry about the things we experienced as kids...I want you to know I forgive you."

God the Father continued to chisel away. In my disgrace, he gave me grace. All that I've been through and what I've put others through, and all that I am yet to endure, is about him, masterfully at work, shaping me more and more into the image of his son.

***

I can identify with Jacob in the Old Testament. He was on his way to the Promised Land. But, in order to get there he would have to go through his brother Esau. He had deceived his brother and stolen his birthright. Now Esau was chasing him down to kill him. If you haven't read the story, then pull up a chair to Genesis 32-33.

The night before their encounter, the angel of the Lord wrestled with him. It was a reminder that our battles in life really aren't with people, they're with God. It was a tough battle, lasting all night, but Jacob wouldn't stop fighting until the angel blessed him.

The angel asked, "What is your name?"

"Jacob," he responded.

"Your name shall no longer be called Jacob, but Israel."

Jacob's name meant *deceiver.* This was the life he had known even into adulthood. But, God chose to change his name to Israel, which means *God will fight for us.*

God used the angel of the Lord to break him in order to use him. And to use him, he had to change his identity. The limp he was left with was to be a reminder of his constant need to depend on God.

The very next day he met up with Esau, and instead of a potential annihilation, there was profound reconciliation. Esau ran to Jacob and they embraced and kissed each other. Can you imagine the emotion they must have felt? After this sacred moment in their family, Jacob said, "I have seen your face, which is like seeing the face of God, and you have accepted me" (33:10).

Just as Jacob had seen God's face in Esau, I too, had seen his face in Roger and Sharon. And, just as Jacob was fit to enter the Promised Land, I ended my fight and got back on the road to continue my journey to the King. Of course, I was given my own limp—to walk in humility and transparency.

What does the face of God look like to you?

CHAPTER 13

Forgiven

As the Lord has forgiven you, so you also
must forgive.

—Colossians 3:13

Jesus often spoke about forgiveness. He made it
a significant part of the Lord's Prayer in Mathew
chapter six. It is as important to life as our daily
food supply and a roof over our heads. Without
forgiveness worship can't happen, marriages can't
survive, and according to Ephesians 4:26, a day
should not end without it.

So, what is forgiveness?

I've learned forgiveness is a *choice*. In Ephesians
4:32 we are commanded to "forgive one another, just
as God in Christ Jesus has forgiven us." Since God
the Father chose to forgive us, so we can choose
to forgive ourselves, and others. Colossians 3:13
affirms: "As the Lord has forgiven you, so you also
must forgive."

When I choose to forgive, I am agreeing with God that I've been forgiven and that the person who has hurt me has already been forgiven on the cross. According to Ephesians 1:7, forgiveness is a part of our spiritual blessings and evidence of our new identity in Christ. When we choose not to forgive, then we're disagreeing with God. We are becoming our own judge, choosing to live in our own world of bitterness in rejection of his truth.

Forgiveness is an unconditional choice. How many times have we found ourselves saying, "If only...If only God could forgive me. If only they would promise to never hurt me again. If only they would come to me and say they were sorry—then I'd forgive."

Often though, offenders, when confronted, are fearful to confess and refuse to acknowledge their actions. The truth is, we should choose to forgive regardless of whether or not the person that sinned against us ever comes forward and admits they have hurt us.

I shouldn't forgive to get my needs met for affirmation or self-worth. I shouldn't hold out in order to get even, or to see that the offender gets what's coming to them. When we forgive there should be no strings attached. I agree with Brennan Manning, a former Franciscan priest, who once said, "God accepts us the way we are and not the way we should be."[15] I know—it's crazy.

If I've sinned against someone, then I need to go to that person and say "I was wrong. I'm so sorry for what I said (or did) to you." There is no need to add, "And, will you forgive me?" That puts undue pressure on the other person. Forgiveness becomes conditional based upon their response.

The individual may be so hurt that they're not ready to forgive. You need to give them permission to deal with their pain so that in time they can come to you and say, "I accept your apology. You're forgiven."

I've also learned that forgiveness is the *cancellation of a debt*. In Colossians 2:13-15, we learn that Christ cancelled our sin on the cross. He paid the debt. The transaction is complete. So, when we forgive, we identify with what the other person did to us and how what they did impacted our life. Then, we release them from having to pay their debt, and we let them go. In essence, we're saying, "You're free."

The best way to reconcile with someone is face to face. However, sometimes circumstances don't allow for that to happen. Perhaps the person has moved; or the person may have gotten married and confronting them could bring more harm. Or, as happens, maybe the person has died.

The next best way would be to write a letter and mail it to the person. As I've shared, personal letters had a powerful impact on my life. If circumstances prevent sending it, the letter can be written, and stored in your private keeping as a reminder of your decision.

"But, wait," you say. "What if I don't want to forgive? I'd rather hold a grudge, instead." I've heard it said that holding a grudge is like allowing someone to live inside your head rent free. That's no fun.

Why is it so hard to forgive? The reasons are many. The sin was too great. We think the offender needs to suffer and get what's coming to them. Besides, it won't do any good—they'll just do it again. And finally, the lie we tell ourselves from which we gain the most satisfaction—if I forgive them, then they win!

Actually though, if I don't forgive, I'm the one who suffers. Unforgiveness imprisons you, and even can cause damaging emotional and physical harm. Forgiveness is really for you. The offending party has already been forgiven on the cross.

In Matthew 18, Peter asked Jesus how many times he should forgive a person. The Lord replied, "Seventy times seven." In other words, there is no end to the number of times. For our own good, we need to have a continual attitude of forgiveness.

Christ then follows with a story about the kingdom of heaven and the king who wanted to reconcile accounts with his servants (18:23-35). One owed him the equivalent of about one hundred and fifty thousand year's wages. It was impossible for him to pay the debt. Hearing that he and his family would be sold to cover the debt, the servant fell to his knees and begged for mercy. Out of pity, the king released him and forgave the debt.

But, when the same servant found that one of his servants owed him about $2,000 (USD), he grabbed him and began choking him. "Pay or else," he said. The man fell to his knees and pleaded for mercy. But, he refused to cancel the debt and put him in prison.

His fellow servants reported the incident to the king, who summoned him and said, "You wicked servant! I forgave you all that debt because you pleaded with me. And should not you have had mercy on your fellow servant, as I had mercy on you?" In anger, the king delivered him to the jailers, where he would remain until he repaid all his debt.

Then Jesus said, "So also my heavenly Father will do to every one of you, if you do not forgive your brother from your heart." This affirms the importance of forgiveness as a foundational kingdom principle.

***

I could tell by the expression on her face that she was extremely upset. When I finished speaking to the group of ladies, she found me in the hallway, grabbed on to my arms like vice grips, looked me in the eyes, and fumed, "I hate you! I'll never forgive you for what you just said in that room." Then, she abruptly let go and stormed away.

Later on in the retreat this same woman (whom I will refer to as Anna) approached me and said, "I need to talk." That's when she spilled her heartbreaking story.

Anna was born in Germany and grew up during World War II. At the age of five, she witnessed from her bedroom window the execution of her Jewish neighbors—some of whom were her playmates.

By the age of ten, an abusive father became too much for her and she tried to run away. But he found her, took her home, and abused her even more. This cycle continued throughout Anna's teenage years.

She talked about feeling dirty and ashamed, and how she lived in constant fear.

"I figured the only way I could escape was to find an American soldier who would marry me and move to the States," she said. In desperation, she did find a soldier, became pregnant, and returned with him to America.

However, Anna's husband ended up being worse than her father. With great difficulty, she told of how he abused their three daughters. "To this day they have not married because of the painful memories," she said.

She looked away, then ominously admitted, "Now you know why I hate men and why I hate God. I will never forgive." I had very little idea of the impact (if any) of our conversation.

Later in the weekend Anna surprised me. She came rushing toward me with her face beaming; much like a child would run excitedly to her daddy's arms with good news.

"During the night, I thought more about what you said and I surrendered to God's grace. For the first time in fifty years, I'm free! I forgave my country, I forgave my father, I forgave my husband, I forgave God, and I forgave you."

A few years later I called Anna to hear how she was doing and to gain permission to tell her story. "I am so excited," she said. "I have a new husband who loves me. And guess what? I've been praying for my Jewish boss. This week I led him to Christ!"

I tell Anna's story to give you hope. Forgiveness is possible, no matter how shameful and ugly the circumstances. Her story is like Joseph's story in Genesis 50:20. "What man meant for evil, God meant it for good." She is living proof that God's grace is always greater! Romans 5:19 declares, "Where sin increased, grace abounded all the more."

I firmly believe if we choose to not forgive, then we will never understand what God is truly like. Nor, will we be able to enjoy him and celebrate sinners coming to repentance.

When we get stuck on life's road and lose our way, then look for the footprints of the forgiving King. Follow him, so that others who come after us will know the right steps to take.

Two times in Luke 15:7-10, we're directed to this amazing, majestic scene where all of heaven is rejoicing when one person confesses and turns from his sin. It's a true reminder that what brings God the most joy is when we allow his grace to break through in our lives.

The Kingdom of Heaven gives the impression that God is less interested with our behavior and more interested in our repentance. Isn't that the sense you get when the prodigal son returns home to his father?

The father represents God. When the father interrupts the wayward son's confession, it's like he's saying, "Don't bother me with all that stuff. Welcome home. Let's have a party!"

Forgiveness is God's faithfulness in action. 1 John 1:9 says, "If we confess our sins, he is faithful and just to forgive us our sins and to cleanse us from all unrighteousness." Forgiveness can only be obtained through open and honest humility (James 4:6). If I refuse to forgive, then I become like the older brother in the story—a Pharisee.

In our journey to the King, I have discovered the power of trusting in his grace to forgive myself and to receive pardon from others. My encounters with grace have proven that God is faithful—that his ways can be trusted. But, we all know that forgiving can be hard, especially when it comes to yourself and the people you love.

Debbie and I would soon face our most difficult encounter with forgiveness. Could the truths we had learned make a difference?

CHAPTER 14

Family Secrets

Many women have done excellently, but
you surpass them all.

—Proverbs 31:29

Having the right person to walk with you on the
journey to see the King is critical. Debbie Ferrell
was the only suitable wife for me. Without her, my
life and ministry would not be complete, or even
possible. Though she has excelled as a faithful
ministry partner, her greatest ministry has been to
her family.

I could not be more thankful that God led me
to the wife of his choice, which begs the question:
When choosing a life mate, what do you look for?
The best wisdom I have found is offered in Proverbs
31:10-31. The question is posed, "Who can find an
excellent woman?" In this a mother helps her son,
King Lemuel, search for a wife who fears the Lord.

This doesn't mean the right woman is non-existent, but that she is rare. Men, when searching for a godly wife, listen to the wise counsel of your mother, and also observe her mother. Mrs. Ferrell was the model of an excellent wife and mother, and I could see this would be true of her daughter. Ladies, when searching for a godly husband, make sure he has been taught to love and treasure his wife.

If you know my wife, you are blessed. Debbie is "far more precious that jewels" (31:10). A big reason why she is precious to me is she takes her calling as a wife, mother, and grandmother very seriously. And because of that, I can fully trust her with the care of our family and home.

My wife functions in such a way as to honor me and my leadership, never denigrating it. She is the perfect fit for me, physically, emotionally, and spiritually. As a noble woman she enhances any goodness in me. Rather than be discouraged about who I was, she sees me in light of who I can become. She knows how to bring out the best in me and everyone who surrounds her.

Debbie is a kind, positive encourager and would daily model this before our children. Each day I came home from work I could count on her and the children waiting at the front door with a smile, to hug me and excitedly welcome me home.

Her smile is infectious. What's the secret behind that smile? The secret is her godly character. As a mother Debbie constantly built into the lives of her family, always thinking more of us and less of herself. At bedtime she would make the rounds to read books or Bible stories to each of the children and pray with them. My wife loves her family unconditionally, and if she has a weakness, it would be that she loves us too much.

Debbie would faithfully rise early to read her Bible, pray for us, and write in her journal about what was going on in each of our lives. While the kids were at school she would get calls from young mothers seeking her advice on childrearing. She faithfully passed on to moms the wisdom she had gained about how to raise kids who would grow up to love and serve God.

My wife would say that motherhood is more than "three hots and a cot." In other words, there was more to having children than cooking three meals a day and providing a roof over their head. For her, motherhood involved many sleepless nights, rocking a baby to sleep as she sang *Jesus Loves Me,* and praying over a sick child. No matter the situation, Debbie could make it a time to teach our kids about God's mighty deeds and faithfulness.

Birthdays were always celebrated in grand fashion. The "Happy Birthday" sign would be hung over our kitchen bay window a few days in advance. Each child could choose a design and Debbie would construct and bake their cake accordingly. Blowing out candles, leading the birthday chorus, opening carefully wrapped presents, and scooping out ice cream brought her much joy.

She had nurtured a little sewing business to contribute to the family income, but her real delight was making clothes for the girls and their baby dolls. (She even made a few of Robby's clothes when he was an infant.)

Debbie was a meticulous seamstress, putting many hours into making Christmas and Easter dresses with all the fancy frills. My wife saved us a lot of money by providing outfits for our children and grandchildren. Later, she would make some of their prom dresses.

Family outings were filled with history trivia. We came to appreciate the gold mining town of Dahlonega and the story behind the Eastern Band of Cherokee Indians. Some of our favorite places to visit were the Cabbage Patch Hospital in Cleveland, Vogel State Park near Blairsville, and old country stores along the mountain highways, where the kids bought penny candy. Other times we enjoyed family vacations to Panama City, Florida and Missionary Acres in Missouri.

We started a tradition of going to North Georgia for an annual family retreat. This would later become a family reunion when our kids married and had children. Cherith researched the best deals for renting a cabin and organized the weekend events. Our favorite place to go was on Lake Nottley, just outside of Blairsville in the North Georgia Mountains.

Easter, Thanksgiving, and Christmas are Debbie's favorite times of the year. She spends days planning and preparing the meals. The dining table would be decorated with flowers and all kinds of festive trinkets. Easter was a good time to share the gospel and tell the kids about Jesus' death and resurrection. She would color Easter eggs with the kids and oversee an entertaining Easter Egg Hunt.

Every Thanksgiving Debbie baked a scrumptious turkey and made sure I had plenty of mashed potatoes and gravy. Her homemade pecan and pumpkin pies were to die for. On the Friday after Thanksgiving it was our tradition to drive to the nearby Blueberry Patch Farms and take a tractor hayride through the fields of Christmas trees. Debbie always made sure we had a family picture taken in the antique sleigh, and then it was off to eating freshly baked funnel cakes sprinkled with powdered sugar.

When it came to selecting our Christmas tree, we'd search for the perfect Virginia Pine and the kids would help me cut it down. Then, we all tied it to the roof of our van and took it home to decorate. Ordering pizza for dinner and eating it while we trimmed the tree brought a memorable end to a fun day.

This also was the time Debbie would get out her recipe books and begin making all of the Christmas goodies. She allowed the kids to join in and decorate the sugar cookies. Christmas music would be playing in the kitchen as I kept a roaring fire in the fireplace. And, she made sure the two of us watched our favorite Christmas movies and Hallmark presentations.

On Sunday evenings in December our family would celebrate Advent and relive the Old Testament prophet's prediction of the coming Messiah and the events leading up to his New Testament birth. We would sit around the kitchen table and read a passage of Scripture, discuss it, sing a Christmas hymn, and then pray together. Advent would culminate on Christmas Day with the reading of Luke 2.

Christmas Eve would find us at church, joyfully preparing for what the morning would bring. Then we'd come home and eat a light dinner prepared ahead of time by Debbie and the kids. After the kitchen was cleaned up, we would meet downstairs by the fireplace to open our stockings.

On Christmas morning Debbie would make a special breakfast that included hot cinnamon rolls. Then, we would each claim our places by the fire and the tree to open presents.

We would go around in a circle, taking turns, opening one gift at a time. It made for a long Christmas morning, but the process definitely brought more meaning. I'd spend the rest of the day assembling bicycles or putting decals on toys.

The holidays wouldn't have been complete if the kids weren't putting together items in shoe boxes for Samaritan's Purse to send to needy children around the world. There also were several times when we were able to purchase groceries and supplies for single mothers.

One of my wife's favorite things to do is to watch the snow fall. She celebrates when flurries turn into snowflakes. We could always count on a few inches of snow a year and the kids and I making snowmen. Debbie enjoys telling guests about what happened on March 12, 1993, when a freak spring blizzard dumped over a foot of snow on the Atlanta area.

Debbie is a frugal, thrifty spender. Every week she faithfully clipped coupons to save on grocery shopping. When purchasing clothes for the family, she checks out the discount racks first. She would rather sew her own dresses, than lavishing on herself.

My wife loved playing the piano and singing with the family. I think she knows every song in the hymnbook and can usually be heard singing to herself while doing household chores. Debbie is never idle. She constantly moves about the house, making sure everything is clean, picked up, and in its place. She despises clutter.

Our family had its share of pets, mostly cats. One time our cat Matilda had her litter under Amber's bed, even though I had provided a "birthing box" in the garage.

We could tell one very small kitten had been separated from the others and was not moving. Before she left for school that morning, Amber crawled under the bed and rescued the little one. After covering it with a small towel she gently massaged it until it was breathing well and ready to eat.

Amber said she used the resuscitation method she had observed in the Disney movie *101 Dalmations*. She chose to name the kitten *Lily*.

Debbie made sure the kids participated in Bible clubs like AWANA (Approved Workmen Are Not Ashamed), Celebrate Summer, and Vacation Bible School. One highlight of our family's spiritual experience was attending the Atlanta Billy Graham Crusade in October, 1994.

But, perhaps the most meaningful moments we spent together were at supper when the kids told us about their day. Sometimes, they unknowingly even shared their hearts and we learned better how to pray for them during the difficult teenage years.

When the kids went off to college, Debbie would call them every day. She even looked out for her five sisters who were now married and scattered about, calling to check on them. Before he died, Debbie's father asked her to encourage them in their journey and she took his last wish seriously.

***

During our years at Fellowship, the pastoral staff and their wives would go on an annual retreat. We heard the personal stories of each family and prayed regularly for one another. Jan Vander Veen, Jeanne Roland, Norma Street, Christy Kallam, Bev Kinsey, Karen Baumgardner, and Carrie Ott became some of Debbie's dearest friends. These women brought the best out of Debbie and fueled her passion to help produce a godly family.

My wife has been a conduit of biblical wisdom in our home, sharing the secrets of having a happy and healthy family. I pray that my grandsons and the generations to come will seek to marry the same kind of woman found in Proverbs 31. Here's what to look for:

The heart of her husband trusts in her...
She does him good, and not harm, all the
days of her life. She seeks wool and flax
and works with willing hands. She is like
the ships of the merchant; she brings her
food from afar. She rises while it is yet night
and provides food for her household...Her
lamp does not go out at night...She puts
her hands to the distaff, and her hands
hold the spindle. She opens her hand
to the poor and reaches out her hands
to the needy. She is not afraid of snow
for her household, for all her household
are clothed in scarlet...She makes linen
garments and sells them...She opens her
mouth with wisdom, and the teaching of
kindness is on her tongue. She looks well
to the ways of her household and does not
eat the bread of idleness. Her children rise
up and call her blessed; her husband also,
and he praises her. Many women have
done excellently, but you surpass them all.
(31:11-29)

I love Debbie very much. She is a great woman.
Yet, most likely my wife will not become famous or
appear on the cover of a women's magazine. In my
eyes, and I believe in the eyes of God, her greatness
was born of her faithful, loving, day-to-day care of
her family and her love and devotion to him.

***

DEBBIE: *Since I couldn't talk Mike out of writing
this chapter, I'll add a few words of my own.*

God knew better than I did what kind of man would be best for me. Oh, I had my list: must love God, must be kind, must have a "wow" factor, etc. But God knew how important other character qualities would be. Mike is very kind and has a gentle spirit. He is very slow to anger (except in traffic, which he is working on) and gives grace almost always, even when people deserve grief.

Now, about all of those kind words he said about me. The cinnamon rolls on Christmas morning are frozen, not homemade. Also, when we got married I was horrified to learn that his family opened all of their gifts on Christmas Eve. My family opened all of ours on Christmas morning. How would we decide which tradition to carry on?

Well, I'd like to say that one of us graciously gave in but that was not the case. We compromised. We did stockings on Christmas Eve. Christmas Day was the tree. I put some of the kid's significant gifts in their stockings so that we could enjoy two days of gifts. I think Mike and I have both been pleased with the result.

My greatest learning experiences in regard to being a wife and mom that pleases God came from the women's ministry of Fellowship Bible Church. It began in September of 1986, and for nearly ten years I sat under the teaching of Pat Harley. She and several other wonderful Bible teachers really taught me what God's Word says on the subject of godly womanhood. Juanita Lott had plenty of practical ideas on how to manage an efficient and fun home on a daily basis. I'll always thank God for their influence on my life.

CHAPTER 15

The Launch

Follow your dream, even if you're the only
one who thinks you should.
                                        —Tim Kallam

During the final years of seminary God had put on
my heart to one day plant a new church. Becoming
the shepherd of a flock was continually on my mind.
That's why coming to FBC seemed so right. The
church's vision was to multiply and plant churches.

I was holding on to the hope that once I gained
some needed pastoral experience, Debbie and
I could be a part of an FBC church plant. Each
year during my review Art Vander Veen, the senior
pastor, wanted to discuss the previous year and any
initiatives I had planned for the coming year.

He was always positive and encouraging when
it came to my ministry. I was so fortunate. Being a
part of a pastoral team that included the likes of Art,
Bob Roland, and Myles Lorenzen, was like working

with the Trinity. The three of them had helped start *Walk Thru the Bible*. It was Art who instilled in me the need to have a purpose statement for my family.

Yet, whenever it came to sharing with Art my desire to one day be a part of an FBC church plant he would hesitate and then graciously express his concern. He thought I didn't fit the profile of a pioneer church planter and that I would best serve FBC in the areas of youth, missions, small group ministry, and pastoral care.

Once a month the pastoral staff would travel to Conyers and spend the night at The Monastery of the Holy Spirit. Tim Kallam, the senior high youth pastor, and I would go for long walks on the grounds and talk about the future. He, too, wanted to lead a congregation one day.

For a time, Bob, Tim, and I each led a third of the congregation. After worship, our Grace Central group would assemble and meet around tables. It was so much fun and was much like leading a small congregation.

Tim was a big encouragement. "Mike, you're gonna have to follow your dream, even if you're the only one who thinks you should," he said. He was right. Although it's what I longed to do, I feared making the decision.

The reason is because it was a pivotal time in our kid's lives and the thought of taking them away from their friends and the FBC youth group was disconcerting to both Debbie and me. The issue wasn't if we should plant a church. The concern was, "Is this the best time?"

I also came to the sober realization that my ministry plans were affecting Debbie. I had put more thought and energy into fulfilling my dreams, rather than considering the wishes of my wife.

When I became aware of my selfishness, I had a change of heart. I surrendered my dreams to the Lord. I figured if he wanted me to plant a church, then he would make it happen. In the meantime, my family became my number one priority.

***

In December, 1994, I met with Art for my annual ministry review. It was the defining moment. Art said, "Mike, this passion you have to plant a church just won't go away. I think you need to pursue your dream." FBC wasn't seeking to plant another church at the time and I knew this meant we would have to venture out on our own.

With resolve, I looked in the mirror and said, "Okay God, what do we do now?" Suddenly, trusting God didn't feel so good.

My precious wife prayed for me, followed me, and trusted that I would lead our family in the right direction. She gave her permission for me to move forward if I would first consider planting a church in the area.

Fellowship was so gracious to us during the transition. I was given six-month's salary and freedom to focus on putting a plan of action together. On our last Sunday the church gifted us with a weekend getaway to the Grove Park Inn in Asheville,

North Carolina. Then the congregation blessed us with a standing ovation.

As we began to pray about a location, the Hickory Flat area kept rising to the surface. We settled on a start-up date of June 1, 1995. One-by-one people came forward to show interest and ask questions. After much prayer and preparation, the day finally arrived. About fifty people showed up for the first service!

Meeting in Jose and Patty DeUrioste's home, we chose the name Cherokee Community Church and put together a leadership team to guide us; that included Jose, Bill Tuck, Lee Eskew, and me. Then, we held four Sunday evening services to explain the blueprint for the church. With a music team in place, things were really coming together.

The atmosphere was incredible. Over the next two months we increased to about seventy-five people. When we outgrew the DeUrioste home, Bill and Suzan Lam volunteered their farm. We gained some new participants when some of the animals would saunter up to the porch to worship with us.

With the church continuing to grow we found an abandoned campground in Hickory Flat with a suitable building for worship. Our families pitched in putting down new carpet and painting the building, inside and out. Dick Park made a valuable contribution, installing the plumbing for all the bathrooms. Fellowship Bible Church donated one hundred folding chairs.

Late summer of 1995 was bittersweet. On August 11th, while we were celebrating our church expansion, my mom died unexpectedly. She had just turned sixty-five in June and was looking forward to retirement. She had stumbled and broken her ankle. Some weeks later a blood clot developed and took her life.

All my siblings and their families, scattered around the world from South Africa to Hawaii, gathered at Missionary Acres for her funeral. Larry, Roger, Sharon, and I spoke during the service. I shared about the greatest lesson my mother had taught me—that it was okay to trust God...no matter what.

In October, the city of Atlanta witnessed a miracle (lol). The Braves finally won a World Series! Some people jokingly quipped, "There *is* a God!"

Over the next year the church steadily grew to more than one hundred people. We ordained three elders and developed awesome Children's and Youth Ministries. We held our first baptismal service at Red Top Mountain State Park. A highlight for me was baptizing Cherith and Robby in Lake Allatoona.

Our church paid for me to do a nine-week discipleship internship at Grace Ministries in Marietta. Tom Grady was founder and president of the training program. I learned so much from him, Jim Walter, Scott Brittin, and James Eubanks about living and serving out of our identity in Christ. This training brought about a major transformation in my life and would become the signature to my ministry.

With both my parents now gone, life took a serious turn. We were next in line. It was completely up to us if we were to continue the McCrum legacy.

CHAPTER 16

Unwanted Detour

Oh, Dear Gussie Petunia!
—Southern Expression

My wife Debbie sometimes uses the phrase, "Oh, Dear Gussie Petunia!" It's a perfect expression for the times we find ourselves in a strange, unhappy situation that doesn't have a simple solution. Between 1997 and 1999, our ministry life was, in a word, *weird*. It felt like we were trying to walk our way through and out of a giant maze.

In late October 1997, my brothers-in-law Lloyd Bedford and Bruce Schneider, along with some men from our church, helped me put a wood floor down in our foyer and kitchen. The old pine planks were leftovers given to us by Bruce Arrendale. This was an unexpected surprise from God.

That same month our family came under intense spiritual attack. Debbie and I went to great lengths to humbly express our regret and offer grace to those involved in the situation. Unfortunately, for some uncanny reason, our sack clothes and ashes appeared to go unnoticed.

The pain was debilitating and our inner beings felt mutilated. What hurt most was the wounds were being caused by people who we held dear.

How does one respond when people throw spears at you? The natural thing to do is defend one's self. Then, pick them up and throw them back from where they came. But, that's not how David responded when King Saul tried to kill him (1 Samuel 19:9). He did not retaliate, nor seek revenge. Instead, he continued to give his master what he didn't deserve—mercy.

When Jesus was on trial, he didn't respond to the threats of his accusers or use his God-given authority to get even with them. He was strangely silent. I was certain my response to our accusers should be the same. I chose meekness and took the hit.

As it became clear that reconciliation was not possible, I decided to do what was best for Debbie and our family. It was very difficult for me, but I chose to resign from the church, step aside from ministry for a season, and help my family heal.

Christmas was almost unbearable that year. Our hearts ached. However, in all our pain God was faithful. He surrounded us with some dear, loving friends who walked along side us during this upsetting time.

On a Saturday morning in January, 1998, Debbie and I were hurting so deeply that I asked her if we should call someone to come and pray with us. We looked at each other and gave the same response: "The Rolands."

I called Bob to see if he and Jeanne could come over. Within minutes they arrived. We tearfully recounted the entire story. Sharing our burden with trusted friends was so important in the process of healing and moving on. Their love, and the love of several others, truly saved us.

Bob invited us to attend Fellowship Bible Church the next morning, and to sit with them. When he met us at the front entrance, I remember asking, "How long will this last?" He turned to me and said, "Until you can trust God through it, and thank him for it." Bummer! I was thinking weeks. God was thinking years.

I would never get over what Bob said that day. Art Vander Veen's timely sermon brought healing to our souls and gave us hope. Wow! God *was* faithful!

A few weeks later I was attending to some business in nearby Canton. As I sat on a bench in front of the building I happened to look out into the parking lot. I watched as a car pulled in to the space right in front of me. The woman driver got out of her car and entered the building.

My eyes were curiously drawn to the license plate on the front bumper. I did a double take. I had never seen such a plate, and to this day I have not come across one like it. It looked like a regular Georgia license plate, complete with the peach logo. It read: 1NCHRIST.

Immediately, I became aware of God's presence. Peace burst on the scene, letting me know that even in the difficult circumstances we were going through, he could be trusted and we could be thankful. The verse 1 Thessalonians 5:18 flashed before me: "Give thanks in all circumstances; for this is the will of God in Christ Jesus for you."

Gary Klingler once told me he thought every pastor should take time away from ministry and see what it is like to work in the business world. This was my opportunity, but, I didn't know where to begin.

Thankfully, Bob Roland stepped in again. He helped me write a one-page resume. Then, I met with businessmen Jim Reese and Dave Emrich to learn how to have a successful interview. I owe a lot to these men.

Dave gave me my first assignment. I was to contact Arol Wolford, the president of Construction Market Data in Norcross and ask for an interview. In the process I learned that Arol was an elder at Dunwoody Community Church.

I put my speech together and practiced delivering it several times to Debbie. I called CMD and spoke with the vice president, Tom Lutz, and he agreed to meet me for lunch. That's when I learned about Arol's desire to help pastors who were between churches, or who had been hurt and felt the need to step away from full-time ministry for a season. I found out there were about ten former pastors currently among their three hundred employees.

My second interview was with Paul Schaefer. He called me a few days later with a job offer. It was for $21,000 a year. *Ouch!* I had just left a salary over three times that. I told him we'd take it. Debbie and I saw it as a gift from God and knew that he would somehow supply the rest.

Making the transition from ministry to the business world was extremely challenging for me. I had to learn advanced computer skills and the sales process so quickly. Many mornings, as I drove an hour and a half to work, I would cry out to God. The motivation that kept me going was to do whatever it took to provide for Debbie and my family.

I was fortunate to have Kevan Sears (a longtime friend from FBC) and Paul as my supervisors. I was given sales training at Tommy Hopkins Boot Camp in Scottsdale, Arizona and actually received the third place award for performance. While at CMD I also had the opportunity to travel to cities like New York and Chicago, giving sales presentations to company executives.

One day Arol came by my cubicle. I stood to shake his outstretched hand. He looked me in the eye and smiled, "I want to thank you for all the accounts you've been renewing. You've saved the company over $250,000." His affirmation was just what I needed. It was like a smile from the Lord. In ninety days my salary rose to $40,000. Again, God was faithful.

***

In the final chapter of the book of Job, after the grueling torment by his three friends, God told Job to pray a blessing on them (Job 42:8). We read that when he did, God blessed him as well.

I learned something valuable from Job's act of humility. Whenever the faces of the people who hurt our family came to mind (which at first was many times a day), I prayed a simple prayer: "Father, bless them. Bless their families." After about six months their faces were no longer there to haunt me.

I was able to practice what Jesus taught us in the Sermon on the Mount: love our enemies, pray for them, and then let them go. I also gratefully experienced the precious truth that forgiveness is God's way to blessing.

Our departure from Cherokee Community Church had been strained, too painful for goodbyes. I initiated a meeting with the previous leaders of CCC to have a sense of closure, and we experienced grace.

In his book, *Facing Messy Stuff in the Church,* Kenneth Swetland writes, "If you don't say 'goodbye' when you leave a church, you can't say 'hello' in the new one. And, if the church doesn't say 'goodbye' to you, they'll never be able to say 'hello' to the new pastor."[16]

***

While I was working at CMD a fellow employee told me about his father's church in Atlanta that was looking to hire a church administrator. I met with Dr. Jim Collins and was deeply impressed with his love for Christ and his shepherding heart. He offered me the position, knowing they needed me and I needed them.

During our nine months at Peachtree Christian Church I developed some of the deepest friendships I have to this day. Bernie and Lori McClure, Todd and Miriam Dolson, Fred Heddinger, and Gary and Cassandra Sheldon brought back energy to my life. I began to feel the call to ministry again.

Peachtree Christian was smack in the middle of downtown Atlanta. A cathedral of sorts, it was a very historic and ornate church with huge stained glass windows depicting Bible stories. It would become a place for me to heal, a safe haven, where I learned more about our gentle Savior from Dr. Collins. He reminded me so much of the True Shepherd.

After six months, Jim met with me and said, "Mike, thank you for all you've done for us—the administration, counseling, and preaching. We love you, but you're not supposed to be here. You're a pastor. You need to lead your own congregation and I'd love for it to be in our denomination (Disciples of Christ)." He went on to say this would mean I would need to be re-ordained in the DOC.

On June 6, Debbie and I sat on our living room couch, discussing our future. We both agreed that God had restored our emotional health and that it was time to start a new church. We decided to go independent, rather than with a denomination. Dr. Collins supported us and even allowed me time to research an area for a church start-up. Once again we were drawn to Cherokee County.

I completed my assignment at PCC in August, 1999, and thanks to Kevan Sears, I was able to return to full-time work at CMD. This meant I would plant the church as a bivocational pastor. We understood how difficult it would be to do both, but believed it was the right course of direction for us.

CHAPTER 17

A Promise Kept

For I know the plans I have for you, declares
the LORD, plans for welfare and not for
evil, to give you a future and a hope.
                                    —Jeremiah 29:11

Learning to trust God became a consistent theme
in our lives. By now two of our three daughters
were attending Columbia International University in
South Carolina. One weekend, Destiny came home
and said, "Dad, it's been a hard semester. But, I
want to thank you and mom for teaching me to trust
in God. Otherwise, I never would have made it."

I made a marriage vow to Debbie on August 15,
1975. On August 15, 1999, I fulfilled a ministry
promise I had made her in June. On that day we
met with a few families to incorporate as Christlife
Church. Our first public Sunday worship service was
on October 19th, at the Cherokee County recreation
center in Woodstock.

The congregation included the Ebbie Taylor family, the Michael Allen family, the Billy McKillop family, the Joe Reed family, the Carder family, the Rick Stark family, the Dave Milliron family, Lee and Kathryn Eskew, Dick and Thelma Park, Annie Parks, and the McCrum family. It was especially a joy to have my sister, Sharon McKillop, at our side.

On December 4, 1999, we celebrated Destiny's marriage to Jeff Howe. I was asked to perform the ceremony. After the exchange of rings, I said to Jeff, "There's one more ring. This is the ring I gave to Destiny when she was a teenager. We made a covenant together. She was to wear this gold ring, and on her wedding day, give it to the one man who was worthy of her. Jeff, you're the man."

Jeff and Destiny have been blessed with four children. Wilfred "Will" Michael Howe was born October 25, 2001, in Syracuse, New York. Madelynn "Maddie" Jean Howe was born March 16, 2003, in Syracuse. Abigail Grace Howe was born May 14, 2004 at Piedmont Hospital in Atlanta. Aiden Waylon Howe was born December 12, 2006, at Northside Hospital in Atlanta.

***

On Sunday morning December 26, 1999, I preached through some pain I was having in my right leg. When I got home from church, I put on short pants and a T-shirt. As I came down the steps to the kitchen Debbie said, "Have you looked at the back of your leg?"

I looked down and saw that my right calf and lower leg was blue and purple in color. Had I bruised it on something? We kept an eye on it and waited until the next morning to call our doctor.

When a sonogram revealed two blood clots, I was immediately sent to the ER at Kennestone Hospital. After an MRI, the doctors determined that the blood clots were the result of a tumor on my left kidney.

With a partial nephrectomy, the renal carcinoma was completely removed. During the same surgery a Greenfield Filter was inserted in my main artery to prevent future clotting. I was told that the blood clots had saved my life.

It was the first week of January, 2000. Even though the world had not come to an end as feared by many, my *ministry* was in question. It would take me over three months to fully recover from the surgery. My supervisor, Kevan Sears, was sympathetic and said not to worry about my job at CMD. It would be waiting for me when I got well. We were fortunate that the company provided good health insurance benefits.

That same month the transmission went out on Debbie's van. She was dependent on it every day to drive Amber and Robby to Sequoyah High School. We waited on God again. He was faithful to provide for my health. Could he do the same for Debbie, and provide a means of transportation?

My friend, Jay Street, called and told me he needed to come over for a visit. When he arrived, he said, "Mike, you better sit down." With a twinkle in his eye, Jay continued, "Someone must love you and

Debbie very much. They want to buy you a brand new van!"

Lee Eskew drove me to Honda Carland in Roswell and I picked out a 2000 Honda Odyssey for Debbie. Now, *that* was a gift!

***

During this period, a couple of families at Christlife Church felt it was time to move on. With only fifteen of us, we moved our Sunday worship service to Slope's Barbecue restaurant in Woodstock. Bob White, the owner, let us rent it for a nominal fee. The place obviously smelled like smoke, and when I spoke, the ice machine would unload.

But, God was faithful. Amber's friend, Brian, trusted Christ as Savior. And with his family looking on, I baptized him in the cold waters of Mountain Lake in Roswell. Another blessing was Dan Landers. He and his wife June moved with Dan's company to Atlanta from Memphis. Dan played the piano for our group.

From there we moved the church to the Roswell Montessori School. This location was just two miles from FBC. Even though we were small, God began creating a real sense of family.

Debbie was a great encourager and enjoyed being a part of a small church. Our children wanted to be involved and they very helpful. Sometimes, Amber would go early with me on Sunday to set up chairs. She and Robby were a part of the music team.

However, I was lonely on the inside. All I knew to do was to just be faithful and not quit.

One Sunday I had gone early to the church. I was really discouraged. I thought, *Why am I doing this?* Just then, the door opened. It was Dick and Thelma Park. They were like a father and mother to us. Dick was always smiling, even though he was getting frail from several heart surgeries and Parkinson disease. The Holy Spirit clearly said, "Do it for them."

I needed help with the Sunday preaching, especially since I was still recovering physically. I contacted Jay Street, at Fellowship, and asked him if he would consider joining with us as a co-pastor. His family said, "We can't let Pastor Mike do this alone. He needs us." The Streets became a huge blessing to me and our family for the next five years. (One day I hope to buy him the biggest steak in Atlanta!)

The church grew to forty people, signaling the need to find another facility. We were fortunate to locate a school building on Arnold Mill Road in Woodstock, less than a mile from our house. King's Academy was more than gracious and let us rent the chapel for $800 a month.

Sunday morning at Christlife began with worship. Then, to apply the message, we would fellowship around tables during the second hour. This became a great time to foster community, while drinking coffee and munching on snacks.

In January, 2003, I preached a message to our flock from the Gospel of Mark, where Jesus said to Peter, "Get out of the boat!" I told our congregation that Sunday that I felt God was getting ready to stretch our faith and give us a greater opportunity to reach our surrounding community for Christ.

***

In 1972, two men knelt beside a pick-up truck with their faces toward a twenty-four acre tract of land located on a winding country road. They promised to give the land to the Lord. Their prayer was that, somehow, this pristine land would be set aside for a church. Eight years later, in God's perfect timing, he was faithful and answered their prayer.

On December 2, 1980, several families began meeting as a small group Bible study at the home of Parvin and Brenda Ledford. On January 10, 1981, the group decided to establish a church and a groundbreaking took place at the property on June 14th. Promised Land Bible Church was incorporated in the spring of 1982.

I first heard about PLBC when my family moved to Woodstock from Dallas in 1986. Our first night was spent at the home of Gene and Eldeen Schrader, who happened to live on Jep Wheeler Road next door to the church property. Gene had helped develop the initial leadership team.

In February, 2003, Randy Moore, a member of the leadership council at Promised Land, contacted me to say they were looking for a senior pastor and wanted to know if I'd be interested. This sounded right. They needed a pastor and we needed property.

I mentioned my conversation with Randy to Debbie and to Jay. Both surprised me in their positive response: "This might be God at work." The elders issued me a call and I agreed to be their pastor on one condition—with the understanding that I could bring our congregation along with me.

I decided to meet with the previous pastor, Lewis Gregory, to get his thoughts on combining two congregations. At the end of our conversation, he said, "Mike, I believe you're the right pastor for Promised Land." We prayed together and then he encouraged me with Jeremiah 29:11. Here's what the Scripture says:

> For I know the plans I have for you, declares
> the LORD, plans for welfare and not for
> evil, to give you a future and a hope.

Both leadership teams agreed to stay intact to maintain unity. For our first Sunday together, we decided on a wedding motif and planned a marriage ceremony between the two churches. The new congregation would retain the name Promised Land Church.

Sunday, September 28, 2003, the two churches merged into one. The local newspaper sent a photographer to record the event. A front page article appeared in the religious section titled, "Holy Union."

The new elder team included Parvin Ledford, Jay Street, Randy Moore, Art Gard, Olan Hicks, Brett Little, and me. Brett became the leader of the team. I was so blessed to serve with this great group of men.

Within six months there were around one hundred people attending Sunday worship. The church provided a full-time salary, making it possible for me to leave CMD.

Our vision was to make disciples and develop new leaders. On the outside there appeared to be a lot of excitement. However, I could see on the inside that the leaders and families of PLBC were tired. Some of the elders had served faithfully for many years without a break. I think they were hoping the new folk from Christlife could instill new life. Instead, the process seemed to be wearing everyone down.

The leaders agreed that changing the name to East Cherokee Community Church would help us better identify with the surrounding community. At first, this seemed to work very well.

The Woodstock Montessori School used the property for a year while their building was being completed. On Sunday afternoons the sanctuary and classrooms were rented and filled with a Hispanic congregation called Fuente da Vida. We held a joint summer Vacation Bible School together, which comprised over one hundred children.

The church property became a new home for Boy Scout Troop 34 and hosted annual Weblorees. We had two major outreaches to our surrounding neighbors and hosted a concert and picnic at the pavilion with over one hundred and fifty people in attendance.

In the spring of 2007, I sensed the need for additional formal training to enhance my pastoral skills. It had been twenty-five years since I graduated from Dallas Theological Seminary. With the agreement of the elders, I applied for part-time employment at Home Depot in Roswell, with the hope it would pay for my school bill.

But, would these changes be enough to keep the church alive?

CHAPTER 18

The Perfect Storm

Dad, I have to talk to you RIGHT NOW!
—Robby

I applied to Gordon-Conwell Theological Seminary, thinking its large, nationally recognized doctoral program would be a perfect fit for me.

I spoke with the Registrar in South Hamilton, Massachusetts and he wholeheartedly agreed that I should pursue my D.Min. (Doctor of Ministry) with them. At the same time, I would complete four additional master's courses for an M.Div. (Master of Divinity) equivalency.

I was accepted into the *Pastoral Skills for the 21st Century* track. After a ton of reading, I started classes in January of 2008 at the Charlotte, North Carolina campus. Over a four-year period we would look at the pastor as leader, preacher, and caregiver. We took what we learned from our course study and class interaction, and integrated it into our ministry environments.

I absolutely loved going to the campus for two weeks each year and meeting as a cohort of twelve pastors. Dr. David Currie and Dr. Kenneth Swetland were the professors who oversaw the classwork. I was fortunate to have Dr. Haddon Robinson as an instructor for my first year. It was like sitting at the feet of Jesus.

God was faithful to provide a place for me to stay during my two weeks in Charlotte. The first year I was blessed by Cor Hoekstra and his family. I stayed the three remaining years with Alan and Paula Cellamare. I could not have met my financial obligations and completed the program had it not been for these folk providing room and board.

I never dreamed I would study for a doctorate and really didn't know what to expect. I read where there are four camps on the way to climbing the summit of Mt. Everest, the world's highest peak. The difficulty of the climb is evidenced in the name of the final stop before reaching the top—the Death Camp. I imagined myself making that impossible trek.

Earning a doctorate was by far the hardest adventure I would ever attempt...and the most rewarding!

***

On May 20, 2008, our daughter, Amber, moved all her belongings into our garage basement. She had lived two miles away in Alta Wood Apartments for several years as she began her career as a registered nurse. Now that her lease was up she wanted to move back home and prepare for her wedding, just five months away.

I happened to be at home that day and knew rain and storms had been forecast for our area. The county in which we live is one of the top five in the US for tornado activity. By late afternoon the front was coming through from the northeast. Glenn Burns on Channel 2 News was giving a weather alert and warned those who lived in the Arnold Mill area to take cover.

Within minutes we were in total darkness. The winds were swirling violently outside. Debbie, Amber, and I huddled by the sewing machine closet near the downstairs.

Where was Robby?

Amber went halfway up the steps and yelled, "Robby, you better get down here! We're having a storm!"

Robby would seldom listen to his sisters. He was upstairs lying in bed, reading. This time he bounded down the stairs and sat nearby us on the couch and kept reading.

That's when the big winds hit. Debbie and Amber covered their ears. Debbie tried quoting a particular Psalm, but couldn't remember the correct verses or where it was found. She ended up combining several Psalms into something that sounded remotely biblical.

The electricity went out and everything was pitch black. There were three or four big booms and the house shook. Then, in a matter of seconds, the winds died down. The storm was over and we had survived.

Curious, Robby went upstairs to check on things. He was back in a flash. His face was white as a sheet.

"Dad, you need to come see what's happened to your bedroom!"

I hurried upstairs to the second level to find that half of the roof was gone. Some fifty-year-old pine trees and a large poplar had fallen on the house. One lay across the bed Robby had been on a few moments before. There were trees on our bed, as well.

Just like a fearful Dorothy opened the door to Munchkin Land, we opened our front door to catch a view. Trees were down everywhere in the cul-de-sac. The air smelled like fresh pine. Then it started to hail.

We went back in the house only to find the ceiling on the first level starting to cave in from all the water and ice. We hurriedly gathered up some priceless items and secured them in a safe place. Amazingly, Debbie's antique-framed wedding picture was unscratched.

Friends and neighbors helped us cover the roof with tarps. Debbie and I decided to spend the night in the house, protecting our valuables. Amber, her fiancé Mitchell, and Robby all went to Los Bravos for dinner...*Lucky!*

At bedtime, as I was lying beside Debbie on a mattress on the living room floor, I remember thinking, *I can't handle this.* I knew what this would mean and the headache it would be to rebuild—right in the middle of my seminary training. I had just received an assignment in the mail that very day from GCTS.

Thank God for State Farm Insurance. We had just added a total rebuild policy two years earlier. I called them and they came out the next morning to give us a check for $2,000 to take care of initial expenses. Because there was damage to the concrete foundation, our house was declared a total loss and State Farm planned to tear it down and rebuild.

During the reconstruction we were provided a three-bedroom apartment in the same complex from where Amber had just moved. What seemed like a disaster turned out to be a huge blessing. We were getting a new house!

One day as I stood in the street watching workers tear down the walls of our home. The Holy Spirit said, "Mike, that's you. I need to tear down some walls inside you and make you new again."

***

On a cool, wet day in July, 2008, I received a phone call from Robby's friend, Tim. "Mr. McCrum," he said, "I'm worried about Robby. He really seems discouraged. He's more down than I've seen him." As his concern escalated, I felt my heart in my stomach. Robby is our only son. He bears the name of my father.

I drove to where he worked, but he wasn't there. I searched other familiar places, but found nothing, no one. It was pouring rain and I finally headed back to our apartment. There in the driveway was his truck. I bolted up the stairs, ran by Debbie, and knocked on his door.

No answer.

I opened the door to find him lying on his bed, staring at the ceiling. When I saw him breathe, I slumped to the floor beside his bed and began to pray, silently. I stayed until I felt it was okay to leave him alone.

Debbie and I knew that Robby was hurting and going through a difficult time. We kept praying and reaching out to him unconditionally. I took him out to lunch and told him about what happened with me and my father, and some of the regretful things I had done. I related how I had struggled with not being able to forgive myself. He listened, but said not a word.

A few months later the Holy Spirit said, "Tell him what you do." I didn't think he would be interested in knowing, but I approached him anyway and said, "Son, would you like to go on a retreat to hear me speak? You'll get to see what I do." With little hesitation, he replied, "Sure." But, the truth is, he later confessed he wasn't very thrilled about going.

On the way to the retreat I told Robby some of what to expect and that I'd be sharing my story. Once we arrived, he looked around at the people he would be with and was not happy. He was dreading the weekend.

Then, something happened. God's Spirit went to work. In the first session I spoke on *Grace*. After I finished, Robby jumped out of his seat and met me at the door.

"Dad," he said, "I have to talk with you RIGHT NOW!"

We went out in the hall and walked toward the exit door. He turned around, grabbed my shoulders, looked straight into my eyes, and said. "I think I know why you wanted me to come on this weekend." He paused momentarily. Then the tears began to flow. "Dad," he said, "I am so sorry for all the hurt I've caused our family."

It was the twenty-first century version of the prodigal son story. Before he could get another word out, I wrapped my arms around him. We hugged for the longest time.

And then I said, "I forgive you, son. Welcome home."

That was a super-sized sacred moment of grace. It's the way God works. He uses the storms of our life to bring about healing and restoration.

When we arrived back home I said to Debbie, "You have a new son!"

There was so much at stake—generations to come would need to know if God is real. Well, God was real that weekend and awesomely answered our prayers.

Since that weekend Robby has been a different person. The changes that have taken place in his life have made a lasting impression on many of his friends. It was during this time that God brought Susan Hickey into his life to encourage him in his journey.

Today, I delight in our closeness. I am overjoyed at how much Robby loves the Lord. My son now serves on the worship team at Revolution Church in Canton.

***

On October 4, 2008, I walked my daughter Amber down the aisle to marry Mitchell Myers. The wedding ceremony was held at East Cherokee Community Church. It brought Debbie and me much joy to see their marriage established in Christ alone.

Snowbird mission trip: Amber, Cherith,
Robby, Destiny. We always wore our
oldest clothes during that week so we
could get as muddy as we wanted.

Mike presenting the gospel at a
house meeting in Romania. To his
left, Interpreter Gabriella, Graham
Sumner, Dr. David Williams.

Cherokee Community Church at the
home of Bill and Suzan Lam, fall 1995.

Mother's Day, 2003 at Promised Land
Church. *Photo by Randy Moore*

Our house the morning after an EF-1tornado touched down in the neighborhood on May 20, 2008.

Care Ministry Staff at Fellowship Bible
Church, July, 2016. From left: Cindy
Spitler, Marilyn Shinn, Bob Roland,
Larry and Dee Goar, Geoff Wiggins, Mike.
Photo by Cindy Rawlings

Destiny and Jeff Howe on their
wedding day, December 4,
1999. *Photo by Chris Berry*

Cherith on her Mediterranean cruise.
Monte Carlo is in the background.
Photo by First Financial Security

Amber and Mitchell Myers on their
wedding day, October 4, 2004.
Photos by Katherine

Robby with his fiancée Susan Hickey
(December 2015), anticipating their
wedding day, October 14, 2016.
Photo by Amber Cather Photography

Our grandchildren April, 2016: Lily
Myers (4), Aiden Howe (9), Madelynn
Howe (13), Ansley Myers (15 months),
Will Howe (14), Abigail Howe (11).
Photo by Tonia Davis Photography

CHAPTER 19

Pit of Despair

You survived the fire-swamp. You must be very brave. But nobody withstands the machine.

—Albino, *The Princess Bride*

I had been looking forward to my third year at Gordon-Conwell. It was time to declare our thesis project. I listened with envy as we went around the classroom and each pastor announced the subject of their writing.

When it became my turn, I confessed that I didn't have a topic. I was embarrassed and disappointed, sharing with my peers that our church was dying and I would be returning to close it down.

With no hesitation, Dr. Swetland beamed, "Great! This is great, Mike!"

I looked at him in bewilderment.

Then he delightfully explained, "You can write it on *Lessons Learned from a Dying Church*." That didn't sound like a topic worthy of writing about, let alone researching.

As I was driving back from Charlotte, I had a conversation with the Lord. "I thought you wanted me to go to back to seminary in order to make me a better pastor?"

I could almost see him turning his face toward me and saying, "And that's exactly what I intend to do—make you a better pastor."

Suddenly, it all made sense. The pages of my thesis exploded in my mind during the four hour drive back to Woodstock. When I arrived home, I kissed Debbie, dropped my suitcase, and ran over to the computer to begin writing.

It wasn't long before the first fifty pages were written. I used an autopsy motif to dissect the church body. The detailed research would disclose the real reason(s) why a church dies. I could see how it could be in God's plan to use my story to help others who might experience the same tragedy.

Writing my thesis was one of the best things I'd ever done in ministry. I researched dying churches in North America. I read what the Bible says about dying institutions—Israel and the Sardis Church.

I crafted a survey with one hundred former and current members of the congregation to learn why they believed the church had died. The feedback I received was very revealing, and extremely helpful to me as a pastor.

The reason we were dying was because we were not fulfilling Jesus' vision to make disciples, who then make disciples. The leadership had become stagnant. The elders were worn out and there was no one to replace them. As a result, our core group became discouraged.

Our congregation shrank to thirty people and we were no longer able to pay a pastor's salary. Ultimately, the elders agreed to close the church and a final date was set for October 25, 2009. On that day we celebrated and thanked God for the memories and miracles. I encouraged the people to scatter and use their spiritual gifts to bless another congregation.

Despite the sadness, it was actually a good day. I announced that Debbie and I would host a small group in our home on Sundays for those who weren't ready to find a new church. The remaining families were told that the church building and property would be sold and the proceeds given to Wycliffe Bible Translators.

***

If I could describe the ministry for me at this time I would use one word—*crucifixion*. When I realized the church was dying, I knew that included me, as well. I came across the book *The Crucifixion of Ministry*, by Andrew Purves. The title of his Introduction was, "Has God Killed Your Ministry, Yet?"[17]

In the book, Purves writes about two times in a minister's life when he or she experiences brokenness. The first usually happens within the first five years of ministry. The second one comes near the end. The latter is the worst experience a minister is asked to endure. If you make it through, then your most effective and productive years of ministry are ahead.

For six months I went through a crucible, a dark night of the soul, a pit of despair. It reached a climax on a men's Tres Dias retreat. During the Sunday morning chapel, my eyes were drawn to the life-size cross up-front. I imagined Jesus on the cross and was reminded of the reality that God the Father had turned his back on the Son. It was so surreal.

Jesus is crying out, "My God, my God, why have you forsaken me?" And I agreed, thinking, *Yes, God, what are you doing? What are you waiting for?*

The Father says, "I'm waiting for him to die. If he doesn't die, then the graves can't be opened, people will die in their sin, marriages can't be saved, and families can't be restored. He has to die."

Then, I saw myself on a cross, crying out to God: "God, what is it you want? What are you waiting for?

He said, "Mike, I'm waiting for *you* to die."

The truth began to sink in. My Father was waiting for me to die, to come to the end of myself, for my flesh to be removed, so that Jesus could do his resurrected work through me.

Sadly, I was guilty of what I call, "The North American Pastor Syndrome." In order to attract people to come to church, and stay, I felt pressure to make the next Sunday's worship experience even better. I realized that this was like an addictive disease. The way of the flesh was wearing me out.

People should choose a church, not based on who the pastor is or who leads the worship. Nor should a church be chosen based on the programs it offers. We should choose a church where Christ is changing lives.

I now understood I had been good at doing the ministry, but when I turned around, no one was following. I blamed others—their ingratitude, their insensitivity, their laziness, their agendas, their backstabbing.

Like Peter on the shores of Tiberias, I scoffed, "Jesus, what about them? Look at all the pain they've caused me."

Then he whispered, "This is not about them. It's about you and me...Do you love me more?"

I knew what Jesus wanted—he was longing to have intimacy with me. No one was following, because I wasn't "abiding in him" (John 15:4). And, because I wasn't abiding, there was no fruit, just dead branches. Jesus needed to cut away the dead material, so I could fully embrace his love, and allow him to love others through me. That's why I had to go through the fire.

***

In the movie, *The Princess Bride*, the albino examines Westley, who is tied down in the Pit of Despair because of his love for Princess Buttercup. As he cleanses his wounds received from fighting the rodents of unusual size, he announces in a raspy voice, "You survived the fire-swamp. You must be very brave. But nobody withstands the machine."[18]

Count Rugen then activates the water powered torture contraption at the lowest setting. Westley writhes in great pain. Calmly, the Count tells his victim that the concept of the suction pump is centuries old. "Really that's all this is except that instead of sucking water, I'm sucking life. I've just sucked one year of your life away."[19]

I similarly felt like God had tied me down to his machine. This involves us being immobilized while he stands by as our selfishness (flesh) is being sucked away through brokenness. And, it is sobering to imagine that it is God who operates the machine.

Jesus said, "Whoever abides in me and I in him, he it is that bears much fruit, for apart from me you can do nothing" (John 15:5). I learned the hard lesson that the secret to ministry (fruit bearing) is intimacy (abiding), and the secret to intimacy is brokenness.

***

I was grateful for my part time job at Home Depot and the health insurance benefits they provided. But, all I could think about was how much I missed being a pastor.

One day when I was in the breakroom the Lord said, "Look up. There's Bo. There's Denise. They're the reason you're here. I want you to be their pastor."

This would be a bit of a challenge, since Bo and Denise admitted their indifference toward hearing the gospel. Bo even jeered at the idea that Jesus was God, that he was crucified on the cross, and that he rose from the dead.

I began to pray for Bo and Denise. My wife joined with me. Our little Hope Chapel that met in our home prayed each week that one day they would believe in Christ. For three years we prayed.

My assignment didn't require (and even discouraged) preaching or witnessing on the job. Instead, it meant joyfully serving my fellow employees, managers, and customers with humility and love— to manifest Christ in whatever way I could.

Over time Bo and Denise became curious. I imagined the day when they would join us on the road to see the King!

CHAPTER 20

Reluctant Professor

You must come speak at our church!
—Pastor Deborah Yoo

In July, 2010, Margaret Turner called me to ask if I'd come and share a part of my testimony at her Wednesday night choir practice at Restoration Church of God in Roswell. She had attended a women's Tres Dias weekend and heard me speak.

Her husband, Walter, was in the choir and came up to me afterward. He happened to be the Chairman of Religious Studies at Beulah Heights University in downtown Atlanta and asked if I had ever thought about teaching.

He struck a chord. I had thought about the possibility of equipping and mentoring ministers someday. He told me to send him my resume and said, "You never know."

In a few weeks Professor Turner called me. It seems a professor was ill and he needed a substitute for the fall semester. He wanted to know my interest right then. I said, "Yes!"

In hindsight, this was one of the best ministry decisions we've made. I was assigned to teach two classes, *Life in Christ* and *Ministry of Paul*. What could be more thrilling than that?

I was driving to the BHU campus in downtown Atlanta to teach my first class when it suddenly dawned on me—*I'll have to tell my students about the church I pastored, and why it died*. I was sure they would be expecting to hear about a professor's successes and not his messes.

I had the students go around the room and introduce themselves. Then, I asked them to tell about their family and the church they attended. When it was my turn, the Holy Spirit said, "Tell them the story about the church dying." Reluctantly, I obeyed and told how our congregation had recently died, and how it felt like God had killed our church.

I was surprised to find my twenty students keenly interested in what I was sharing. After I finished, there were many questions about my circumstances. One pastor came up during the break and said, "Professor, you don't know what it meant to me to hear you share your story. I've had to close down two churches in the last six months."

As I drove home that first night I was humbled before the Lord. I now knew why I had to experience that awful chapter in my life. God had called me to himself in order to change me, so I could empathize with others. He wanted to equip me to help them know how to navigate through the difficult journey of ministry.

***

I finished my thesis project on time and graduated from Gordon-Conwell on May 20, 2011. It meant a lot to me to have Billy Graham's signature on my diploma, and to see Leighton Ford in the graduation audience. I'm glad my friend Norm Yeater and I were able to finish and be hooded together. Norm would die in a tragic car accident a couple of years later.

I continued to teach at BHU and thoroughly enjoyed being an adjunct professor in a multi-ethnic environment. One Christmas, Debbie and I invited my students to a Christmas holiday dinner in our home. We had the best time! There were several who commented that they had never been inside a professor's home.

I had discovered my gift of teaching and absolutely love it! After I received my doctorate the school asked me to teach in the master's division, as well. For the first time in ministry I felt my audience was listening to me and growing from my teaching.

One of my ministerial students, Bobby Young, paid me the ultimate compliment. "Professor, we take what you teach us in class and teach it to our congregations on Sunday."

An additional benefit has been to serve alongside President Benjamin Karanja and my fellow professors. Professor Dennis Malone has become a dear brother and a tremendous encouragement. We first met when we served together on a Tres Dias weekend. He was the very first to urge me to write.

***

Lily Lynn Myers was born to Amber and Mitchell on October 10, 2011, at North Fulton Hospital in Roswell, Georgia. One week after her birth came the unexpected death of Mitchell's mother. We grieved with the Myers family for their loss. During the same time Cherith was encouraging Amber in the celebration of new life.

***

On January 11, 2012, I began teaching *Revelation* to a class in the graduate program. A Korean student by the name of Dongsup Kwak was placed in my class because the Korean-speaking course wasn't being taught that semester.

As is now my custom, the first day I shared the story about how our church had died and the lessons learned from it.

After class, Dongsup came up to me and said, "Professor, you must come speak at our church." I shared my appreciation for the invitation and told him I was honored. But, due to my heavy workload, I humbly declined.

The next week Dongsup approached me before class and said his pastor told him to tell me, "You must come speak at our church!" By now, I felt compelled to accept her request. What harm would it do? But, when he told me his pastor wanted me to come speak the upcoming Friday night, at 8:30 p.m., I panicked.

Pilgrim's Church is a Wesleyan group with around sixty Korean worshippers, mostly young men and women. Pastor Deborah Yoo and her husband, Yong Kyun Cho, moved from South Korea to Atlanta to pray for the spiritual revival of this country and to start the church. They also managed to get degrees from Vanderbilt University.

Not having time to prepare as I usually would, I pulled out a sermon outline from the past and reworked it some. On the forty-five minute drive to Duluth the Holy Spirit said, "You're not going to preach that message are you? When are you going to ask me what I want you to preach?"

I realized he again wanted me to tell the story of how our church died. I argued my case. This was my first exposure to this church. There would already be a language barrier. Besides, what possible benefit would there be by telling my story?

The congregational singing and choir music were very moving. Then, it was my turn. I preached on the Sardis Church in Revelation 3, and shared how, in a similar way, our church had died.

After the message Paul Cho, the pastor's son, interpreted my sermon into Korean. Pastor Deborah then came to the pulpit. She spoke to the congregation in Korean. I saw her pause after a few remarks and begin to tear up.

I thought, *Oh no, I must have said something wrong. Had I offended them?* She gestured for her son, David, to sit beside me and interpret as she continued to speak to the congregation.

Pastor Yoo shared that during the past year she felt their church was dying and prayed that God would send someone to encourage them. After hearing my message, she knew I was the one. She talked about the sacrifices her family had made in moving to Atlanta to fulfill God's will. Now, with renewed faith and courage, she could continue to pastor the church.

Pastor Yoo asked me to come back to the pulpit and give the closing benediction. I bowed my head and prayed. When I finished praying, I looked out at the congregation and, at first glance, it appeared everyone had left. I thought, *Where did they go?*

As I stepped off the platform and neared the front pew, my eyes were drawn to the people on their knees, between the pews, quietly praying. I was humbled.

It was about 10:30 p.m. when Pastor Yoo turned to me and smiled. She said, "You must go now. We will stay and pray all night. You must come speak again next week." She handed me an envelope and inside was a very gracious financial gift.

During the next six months I spoke at the church nearly every Sunday. Each week they gave me a financial gift that helped us tremendously. It was God's timely faithfulness again. He was blessing their congregation and they began to add new members. Pastor Yoo soon started Pilgrim's

Theological Seminary and I was asked to serve on the school board.

This chapter in our life came as a very delightful surprise. What else could God possibly have in store for us?

CHAPTER 21

The Toilet Aisle

He who began a good work in you will bring
it to completion...

—Philippians 1:6

I was working part time at Home Depot, teaching
courses at BHU, and preaching at Pilgrim's Church
to make ends meet. I also started raising financial
support in order to join the counseling team at Grace
Ministries by May.

By the end of April, 2012, Debbie and I were at
the end of our funds. We had used all our retirement
money, savings, and emergency fund to survive.
On the last day of the month we were down to our
last few pennies. We looked at each other and said,
"Well, what's God going to do this time?"

Normally, I worked with Denise in the paint
department at Home Depot, helping customers with
their paint supplies. Part of my job was to match
colors of various objects that people would bring

in to the store. The most challenging color I had to match was from a leaf that had fallen in a lady's backyard.

However, when I went in to work on May 3ʳᵈ, I was assigned to work in the plumbing department. This was a bit challenging for me because my plumbing skills are limited. It seemed like every time I was asked to cover that department, I could count on getting the toughest customers.

I would be confronted with, "What's wrong with you?...Of all people, you should know how to fix my problem!...It's about this long, it attaches to this, bends down to this, and works like this! You know!"

So, here I was, all by myself on the toilet aisle, when I looked up and saw Bob Roland, the Family Ministries Pastor at Fellowship, coming toward me. It wasn't a surprise to see Bob. We'd been friends for twenty-six years. He would usually come by on his days off to get supplies for the various and sundry projects Jeanne had him working on around the house.

But, this was a Thursday, and what was surprising to me was the way Bob began the conversation. "Mike, I've been looking all over the store for you. I went to the paint department and you weren't there. So, I left the store and was starting to get into my truck, when something told me to turn around and go back in to try one more time."

"I came to find you because God put it on my heart to ask you a question. Now, I don't know if this is something you'd be interested in, or if you could somehow work it into your schedule, but—I

173

interrupted, "Bob, what is it?! What are you trying to tell me?"

"Well, I want to know if you'd consider coming to Fellowship to serve on staff as our temporary Care Ministry Pastor. Now, it's only for six months, until we can hire a permanent pastor. We know who we want and what we're looking for."

"Does it pay?" I said with a cautious smile.

"Yes. It will be the same salary as the previous pastor." Bob continued, "Go home and talk it over with Debbie. But, I need to know your answer in five days."

When I went home and told Debbie I had a job offer that day she said, "From who—another department at Home Depot?"

I calmly responded, "No. It was from Fellowship Bible Church."

"What!" Debbie could hardly hold back her emotions. "Tell me about it!"

I replayed my conversation with Bob and said, "What do you think?" Her reply was an emphatic, "If you don't take the position, I will!"

A few days later, I phoned Bob and said, "You got us!"

As I turned into the church parking lot on my first day, I surveyed the surroundings. I had been here for almost ten years and then gone for seventeen. I said, "Lord why do you want me to come back?" He said, "I'm coming to do a work at Fellowship and I want you to be a part of it."

Because of Dr. Crawford Loritts' expositional approach to preaching, the church had grown to a weekly Sunday crowd of over two thousand. My role would be to provide pastoral care, hospital visitation, counseling, and oversight of several support ministries.

My Administrative Assistant, Lisa Montgomery, made sure that I got off to a strong start. I dove right in and worked hard. It seemed like I'd never left. We quickly renewed old friendships and began to establish new ones.

I had wondered if the elders and pastors had the same passion I had—to make Jesus, not programs, the main focus of the church. I found out within a few weeks where FBC stood on the centrality of Christ. There were two confirmations that made me even more excited about returning to Fellowship.

Elder Brian Dodd spoke at a staff meeting on July 25th about the *Fifteen Common Threads of Prevailing Churches*. He had researched the top seventy-five churches in America and reported that the number one thread for all the churches was, "Jesus, Jesus, Jesus, and when you are done talking about Jesus, talk some more about Jesus!"

In another staff meeting Dr. Loritts shared from his heart. He had just returned from a speaking engagement and revisited his teaching on the book of Philippians. He spoke with passion about how Christ was the center of each chapter.

He reminded us of key verses like "He (Christ) who began a good work in you will bring it to completion at the day of Jesus Christ" (1:6). The Apostle Paul exhorted, "For to me to live is Christ, and to die is gain" (1:20). The climax was my favorite verse: "I can do all things through him (Christ) who strengthens me" (4:13).

In July I had my ninety-day review with Bob. Right up front I said, "Bob, we've got a problem. Debbie and I are getting close to the people and the people are getting close to us."

To which he replied, "Oh yeah. I could see how that could be a problem." Then he added, "Mike, the staff really enjoys working with you and sees you as a good fit. Would you ever consider staying permanently?"

I responded, "Bob, of course! We love Fellowship."

"Well, that's great!" Bob continued. "I'll talk to the elders and staff. I think this can work."

I said, "Bob, wait a minute. I thought you told me this was temporary, for six months, and that you knew who you wanted."

He said, "That's true, Mike...and *you* were the one we wanted!"

When I told Debbie about our conversation she was overjoyed. We both felt that coming back to Fellowship was like arriving at an oasis after a long, weary journey in the desert. This was no mirage. God had provided beyond our wildest dreams!

My position became permanent on October 1, 2012. I wrote my letter of resignation to Home Depot and turned in a two-week notice to my manager.

On my last day there I gave a goodbye letter to Bo and Denise along with a DVD called *The Case for Christ* by Lee Strobel. In the letter I thanked them for our friendship and for letting me work with them the past five years.

At the end of the letter I wrote, "My heart's desire is that you would come to know the same Jesus I know. Here's my phone number. Call me if you ever want to talk about it."

As I passed the electrical aisle on my way out the main entrance, Bo stopped me. Evidently, he had gone to the employee's room and read my letter. He grabbed me by the arms, looked right into my eyes, and said, "Mike, I need to know. Are you sure what you believe about Jesus Christ is true? Are you absolutely positive?"

I said, "Bo, yes, it's true." We hugged and I walked out of the store—still hopeful.

***

In November I received word that our long-time British missionary partner, Graham Sumner, had died. George Deuel, Marye McKinney, Pam Daniell, and I flew to London and on to Cornwall, to the city of Redruth, to comfort his wife, Joy, and her family.

The memorial service was very sacred and meaningful to each of us. We all had been with Graham on several mission trips. While it was sad to see our inspirational leader leave us, we were, on the other hand, rejoicing that he was with the Lord.

The congregation celebrated his home going. I read a passage in John 14 where Jesus tells his disciples he will not leave them as orphans. He would come to them. Graham's three sons were alone now, but God would care for them.

George and I had the opportunity to visit Gwennap Pit, an abandoned copper mine, where John Wesley preached eighteen times between 1762 and 1789. I stood on the platform from which he spoke. The amphitheater was circular, spiraling downward with seating for about five hundred people.

When I returned home to Atlanta I had two messages on my cell phone. Both were from Bo. In the first message he was frantic. "Mike, please call me when you get this message. It is extremely important that I talk to you!" The second message echoed the first. I wondered what may have happened to Bo. *Did he have an accident? Was he okay?*

I called him immediately. He thanked me over and over for calling him back. He said, "Mike, I'm so glad you called. The reason I wanted to talk to you is to say that I'm ready to begin my journey with Christ!"

I excitedly replied, "Really? That's great!"

He wanted me to meet with him, discuss the Bible, and teach him how to pray. The emotion that passed between us was *electric.*

As the conversation wound down, Bo said, "Mike, isn't it incredible that something so amazing and wonderful could come from the electrical aisle at Home Depot?" I knew then that my friend's decision to trust Christ was real.

Bo began his faith journey at the same time his daughter was taking her first steps to recovery from alcohol addiction. I've spent some very meaningful moments with Bo and his family. When we were going through our tragedy, he was there to offer support.

It has been so amazing to watch God work in Bo's life. Once an agnostic, now a child of the King!

CHAPTER 22

Unshackled

...When his heart and mind and life were
unshackled.
—Jack O'Dell, *Pacific Garden Mission*

On February 21, 2013, Debbie and I received a letter
from Ken Moon, the administrator at Missionary
Acres. He was inviting us to their 50ᵗʰ Anniversary
celebration. Since my dad was the first administrator,
they would be honoring him, along with other
missionaries who were there in the beginning.

Larry, Roger, Sharon, and I contributed funds
to have a marble bench engraved with my dad's
quotation and mom's favorite verse. It would be
placed as a memorial on the Walk of Faith sidewalk
trail.

Over the past fifty years there had been eighty-
five missionaries make Missionary Acres their
retirement home. Hundreds of volunteers had helped
make this community a reality. Construction and

maintenance specialists, as well as church youth groups, came from all over the country to help.

My sister Sharon and I drove to Missouri to attend the three-day celebration and participate in the festivities. Dr. Gary Anderson, President of Baptist Mid-Missions, was the keynote speaker. We were asked to share our testimonies in one of the sessions.

There were many out-of-town guests, including Dave and Dotty Seldon and their daughter Rebecca. Of course, Dave and Pat Warren drove down from Cedarville, Ohio to be with us.

One of the highlights was hearing a presentation about the Reverend Roy Emerson, who had sold the property to the mission in 1962. They surprised us with an old radio recording of *Unshackled,* featuring the younger Roy Emerson, a man who, while heavily into alcohol, left his young wife, only to return when he trusted Christ as Savior.

During the first few years of our marriage, Debbie and I had listened to the radio program *Unshackled* every day. It was a production of the Pacific Garden Mission in downtown Chicago. Every program presented a powerful, true story about how a man or woman had been set free from the shackles of sin.

The drama format was created by Harry Saulnier in the style of the "Golden Age of Radio" and first aired in 1950. Jack O'Dell, a professing agnostic and alcoholic, happened to be listening and had the thought, *God, who can change lives...*

Amazingly, Jack gave his life to Christ and would become the director and producer of the program for the next forty years. He would begin each broadcast by dramatically introducing the main character and then stating that he (or she) was transformed, "When his heart and mind and life were unshackled."[20]

This thirty-minute radio program continues to be heard around the world, over fourteen thousand times a week, and in fifteen different languages. The life-changing stories transcend time and continue to change hearts.

It was wonderful to see God bring so much good out of one man's life. It was all because Reverend Emerson was obedient and faithful to him. Years before, he had responded to the call to ministry and moved to the Silva area to establish New Testament Baptist Church. Many years later we were enjoying the fruit of his ministry. What a glorious day!

I went by the old White Hollow school house, and drove by the spot where Elmo's store stood. I walked around the lake at Missionary Acres. I went by the house where I trusted Christ as Savior and where my mom had raised me.

I sat in the Sunday school room where my friends and I had made fun of Miss Grace Lamar. Then, I took the same walk down the gravel road to her house that I had made on that Christmas Day so many years before.

I walked by the garage where my dad was killed. I visited the gravesites where he, my mother, and granddad and grandma McCrum are buried. I remembered the pain I had caused them, and others, during my childhood days.

I visited with Bill and Shirley Hollida in their home and drove past the town of Greenville, where I attended high school. I found the sawmill where some of my basketball teammates had trusted in Christ. And, I stood in the same pulpit when Ron and I had led a youth revival.

There were so many memories racing through my mind. This is where my faith began. And, despite the pain and sorrow, this is where seeds of trust were planted and where it began to grow.

I was thankful to have been raised around missionary families and to see them live out incredible journeys and adventurous stories of their own. Deep down, I admired them and wanted to someday emulate them. To have been a part of God's work and celebrate fifty years of his grace and glory was a monumental blessing.

***

In mid-July I dropped by Home Depot to check up on Denise. A worker told me she was not there that week due to a death in the family. When I got back in my car I realized I had saved her phone number in my cell directory and gave her a call.

Sadly, her life partner, Mark, had died that very week and the funeral was to be held on Saturday, July 20th at All Saints Catholic Church. I grieved with her over the phone and assured her I would attend the service.

The following Wednesday Denise emailed me. She wrote about how sweet it was to look across the church pews during the funeral service and see me sitting in the audience. She thanked me for my support at this difficult moment in her life.

Denise concluded by sharing this incredible news: "So, I just wanted to let you know that I have asked Jesus into my heart. Despite my wobbling faith, I am saved, by the grace of God. I truly desire to know him in a personal way, and so I am on the path, as I have been for some time now."

***

That fall, Bob Roland and I made the decision to address the wave of sexual addiction that was overtaking marriages in the world, as well as in the church. We met with Troy Haas, associate pastor at First Baptist Church in Woodstock and director of Restore Hope to discuss a strategy.

He spoke about the major impact his ministry was having on restoring families in the Atlanta metro area. We discussed the potential of partnering with them and other large churches to attack the problem with full force.

I did a lot of research on this issue and the incredible destruction it has caused. Sexual addiction had become a raging fire that was out of control. I wasn't interested in trying to put the fire out with a squirt gun approach. It would take a network of churches to become spiritual fire hydrants to help extinguish the blaze.

Bob and I prayed and prayed. God made it clear, almost every week, that he was at work and was bringing hope to the Christian marriages in our church that were affected by this disease.

We settled on a partnership with Restore Hope (now known as Hope Quest) and Bob asked me to oversee two support ministries at Fellowship— *Walking Free* and *Journey*. The former would help men who were battling sexual strongholds and the latter would be for women and wives impacted by struggling men.

I told Debbie about the new venture and asked if she felt we could handle such a vital ministry. Her response was, "Absolutely! We must help save these marriages."

I knew what this meant. I would be going behind enemy lines to rescue husbands, wives, and children from spiritually burning homes. But, being in the line of fire, helping families in crisis is the work the Lord has given me to do.

There have been casualties, but there also have been tremendous victories!

CHAPTER 23

Snowmageddon

People were abandoning their cars and knocking on doors of strangers to take them in.

—CNN Reporters

On January 28, 2014, a winter storm warning was issued for North and Central Georgia. Most of the six million people in Greater Atlanta heard the news, but schools and businesses remained open. The television newscasters were only predicting an inch or two of snow. No problem.

I had gone to meet my friend Bob Breneman for lunch at El Jinete, near the intersection of Highway 92 and Sandy Plains Road. There were a few flurries as we settled down to eat Mexican food.

About halfway through our meal we noticed the snow was coming down steadily and that the parking lot was covered. I made the decision to drive the five miles home before things turned worse. However, on the way, the conditions deteriorated rapidly. Cars had begun to lose traction and slide across the highway out of control, landing in roadside ditches.

I inched along ever so carefully, making it home two hours later.

The situation was becoming a disaster. Everyone had decided to leave work at the same time. Schools were closing and buses were getting caught in the maddening traffic. The entire metro area was in gridlock. The interstates came to a standstill. It seemed like the world had come to a complete stop!

During the turmoil, a joy-filled story played itself out. A baby girl named *Grace*, as in "By the Grace of God," was born on the side of Interstate 285 at 5:20 p.m. with the help of one of Atlanta's finest.[21] The family got stuck in traffic and couldn't make the normal fifteen minute drive to the hospital.

We tried to contact our children and to check on their situations. Cherith worked in Norcross, the farthest from home. The trip home usually took her an hour and a half, one way, during rush hour. Even though I warned her to leave immediately, she wasn't able to leave First Financial Security until 2:00 p.m.

I spoke by cell to try and guide Cherith home. The chaos made traction almost impossible. As the night grew dark, people began to abandon their cars and were knocking on the doors of strangers to take them in. Businesses like Kroger and Home Depot welcomed in stranded drivers. Churches opened their doors for food and shelter.

By midnight, Cherith had driven only half way home. I told her to pull over at the next Kroger and spend the night. I didn't hear from her again. At 3:00 a.m. I finally gave in to sleep, hoping and praying she would be safe.

Destiny was trying to get home on Interstate 575, but the traffic had stopped. The city work crews weren't equipped for a shutdown like this. She was finally able to maneuver over to a Waffle House Restaurant. The place was packed with stranded travelers. Robby tried to get out and rescue Destiny, but it was no use. He ended up having to stay overnight with a friend.

The next morning we received a call from Cherith. God had protected her and provided a place to spend the night. She was able to make it to the Roswell Kroger at the corner of Mansell and Crossville Roads.

She landed in the supermarket along with a hundred others. They all made beds in the aisles and used packaged paper towels for pillows. She listened to music and wrote in her journal what she was thankful for—her family, God, her church, her work, and her friends.

By that afternoon she still was not able to drive home. All the highways had been closed. The only way to get through was with a four-wheel drive truck. Fortunately, Amber's husband, Mitchell had one! Amber and her daughter Lily were already at our house, so Mitchell was able to pick up Cherith on his way in to work.

When he found her waiting outside by her car, he jokingly said, "Hey Cherith, do you mind if I go in and do some shopping?" Cherith was ready to clobber him. They left her car there and drove home.

After hearing everyone's dramatic story, we were all so glad to be back together as a family.

***

The first weekend of April I drove to Greenville, Missouri to attend my high school class reunion. It was a quick trip—up one day and back the next. I had a short speech planned. But, when I got there for the luncheon and started mingling with my classmates, I realized they just needed someone to listen to them share their hurts and pains.

I listened as Jeff White brought me up to date on his job and family. I talked with Eddie Johnson, Steve Stroup, Linda (Bagwell) Wissmann, Pat (Meloy) Rainwater, Randy Shell, and others. At first, I remember marveling at how old I felt; then youthful memories made me feel more at ease.

I was about to leave in order to arrive back in Woodstock by midnight, when Sheri (Hughey) Kennedy walked in. We quickly exchanged greetings and then I left.

On the drive home I found myself a little frustrated. "God, I came all this way out of obedience to you. Is this all that you wanted?"

He said, "No Mike, I brought you here for a reason. In time, I'll let you know why."

When I arrived home there was a message on my cell phone from Sheri. I called her right away. She was sorry we weren't able to talk more at the reunion and needed prayer for something she wanted to discuss.

I was able to share about a new ministry we had started to hurting men and women, and help her think through what she should do in her family situation. She said, "Mike, little did we know when we were classmates in high school that we would meet again years later to help bring a solution to a significant problem."

That same month the FBC men's retreat was held at Simpsonwood, a Methodist retreat center, in Norcross, Georgia. The event had been in the planning for over two years and there were more than one hundred and fifty men in attendance.

Our goal was to address the critical needs of manhood—purity, family, and intimacy with God. Troy Haas was one of the keynote speakers. He addressed the men about the devastating effects pornography and sex addiction has had on today's marriages.

At the conclusion of the conference we challenged those who were struggling in this area, and who wanted help, to attend *Walking Free,* which would kick off May 1st. More than thirty men registered!

Starting on a Thursday night, we were able to offer a lot of hope to those fighting for their life, and for their marriage. It's a difficult journey and recovery can take a long time.

In his book, *What Good is God?*, Phillip Yancey keeps sexual addiction in perspective: "God's grace can heal, but it isn't easy to be healed."[22]

Even though our first meeting was very sobering, it was also very special. I remembered the first thoughts I had when I drove into the church parking lot two years earlier. Jesus had truly come to Fellowship!

CHAPTER 24

The Great Sadness

She's not here. She's gone...
—Destiny

On April 29, 2014, I dropped Cherith off at the Atlanta International Airport to catch her flight to Rome. I wrapped my arms around her and gave her a big hug. Then, I looked her in the eyes and said, "I love you, Cherith." Little did I know these words would be the last she heard from me.

Like the sunrise of each new day, God had been faithful to our family over and over again. His mercies had never, ever failed us. Every day, and in every circumstance, his grace had always been sufficient.

But, if there ever was a time I needed to know God's grace was sufficient, it was in the early morning hours of May 6th.

I was jolted to reality by the 3:00 a.m. phone call from the ER doctor. Debbie was in the bedroom trying to sleep. As I hung up the phone, I wondered how I would be able to tell my wife the devastating news.

There was no time to think about the right words to say because Debbie came out of the bedroom and asked, "Who called?"

I collected myself and told her she needed to sit down. I choked back a deep breath of air that tried to beat me to my answer. "It was the hospital," I replied. "Cherith is with the Lord..."

We tried to fight back the tears, but it was no use. We were experiencing a parent's worst nightmare. I had lost a father and mother, but I didn't know how much it would hurt to lose a daughter. Oh, how my heart ached. It felt like it had been physically ripped in two.

I then told Debbie that despite the incredible loss, something strange had happened, something that undeniably revealed God's mercy. "At 2:30 a.m. I was awakened with the awareness of the presence of the Lord. I knew it was him because he put his tender arms of compassion around me, and held me. He kept assuring me that everything would be okay."

Debbie looked at me from across the room and said, "You, too? I peeked over at the clock and it read 2:30 a.m. I was overcome with this great peace and awareness of God's love, assuring me I was safe and that everything would be okay—no matter what!"

We sat in stunned silence. How could this be—tears of sorrow mixed with tears of joy?

Then Debbie spoke. "I always said that if something like this were to happen to one of my children, that I would dig a hole in the backyard, climb inside, and cover myself up with the dirt. There would not be any use to go on. But, now I have this incredible hope."

In those sacred moments we were surrounded by hope. We embraced the promise of Romans 15:13. "May the God of hope fill you with all joy and peace in believing, so that by the power of the Holy Spirit you may abound in hope."

***

It was determined that Destiny and I would take the first Delta flight out of Atlanta to New York City. Around 5:00 a.m. Destiny's husband, Jeff, drove us to the airport and we found a place in the passenger terminal where we could wait quietly until our flight boarded.

I called Debbie at 8:00 a.m. to let her know we were okay and that our plane would soon be boarding passengers. By the sound in her voice, I knew she was hurting, but holding on to God's grace. Amazingly, Jeanne Roland had already showed up on our doorstep at 7:20 a.m. to comfort her.

I called Amber to give an update and to tell her I loved her. I knew the hours ahead would especially be hard on her.

Then, I looked over at Destiny. As a critical care nurse, she had been in traumatic situations with patients before. But, this was different—her very own sister. Her expression was somber and tears beaded as they ran down her sweet face.

We boarded the plane and prepared for the flight to JFK. Up to this point, I felt I had to wear the pastor's hat, doing what I always had done with others in dire need. I now took off the hat and became a father.

Upon arrival, we deplaned and walked the same corridor Cherith had walked just a few hours before. We went straight to find a taxi and headed for Jamaica Hospital in Queens.

When we arrived at the ER, nurses were coming and going. They were much focused and working frantically. We could see that Cherith was hooked up to all kinds of monitors and that she was breathing, but not on her own. I walked over to her lifeless body and looked into her face, hoping any moment she would open her eyes.

Destiny went to find a doctor to ask if she could see the x-rays. A few minutes later she returned and confirmed the final report. "Dad, it was a large mass on her brain. She's not here. She's gone..."

***

During the night, God had surrounded us with tangible expressions of his steadfast love! Theresa Blakey had tirelessly stayed at Cherith's bedside. Destiny's in-laws, Steve and Ellen Howe, drove from upstate New York to be there with Cherith until Destiny and I could make it to the hospital ourselves. At the same time, Karl and Susie Swope (Debbie's sister) drove all the way from Pennsylvania to console us.

In the late morning hours, Phil and Debbie Gerlicher, CEOs of the company where Cherith worked, called us from Atlanta. They were in disbelief, having been on the cruise with Cherith. Phil, without hesitation, said they were catching the next flight to be with us. When they arrived, we collapsed into their arms.

The hospital staff came by to present us with a handmade quilt, crafted for families who experience the loss of a child. A representative from the New York Donor Network appeared and we filled out the paperwork for them to keep the body for a few days to provide organs to others. Cherith had generously signed the back of her driver's license to do just that.

By afternoon, Destiny and I were beginning to think about getting our tickets for the flight home to Atlanta. Robby called to say that his friend, Harry Wolle, who plays guitar on the worship team at Revolution Church in Canton, had arranged for us to use some of his frequent flier miles.

***

Just before 3:00 p.m., Destiny and I surrounded Cherith's bedside and whispered in her ear that we loved her. I kissed her face and stroked her hair. I felt so helpless—there was nothing I could do for her. I will always remember how painful that moment was. The tears wouldn't stop flowing.

Destiny called Debbie at home. By now, she, Amber, Robby, and his fiancée, Susan, were all together. She put them on speaker phone and they all voiced their goodbyes. Then, in a chaotic ER in Queens, New York, we all sang *Great is Thy Faithfulness*—just in case she could hear us.

At 3:30 p.m., Cherith's life on earth was officially completed.

The hospital assured us that she would be well taken care of and that in a few days her body would be brought back to Georgia. Destiny and I were exhausted and decided to leave and catch the next flight back to Atlanta. Karl and Susie were kind enough to drop us off at LaGuardia International Airport.

On the flight home I kept thinking about Debbie and how sad she must be. I prayed that God would give us strength to walk the path of grief ahead.

CHAPTER 25

Waves of Mercy

His mercies never come to an end; they are
new every morning...

—Lamentations 3:22

The book of Lamentations was written in the form of
funeral dirges. These profound words of lament were
inspired to comfort the Jews who were suffering the
loss of their loved ones. Even though God allowed
their war atrocities, Jeremiah continued to remind
the people that they could always count on his
steadfast love.

Debbie and I believed we had the same God.
Despite our constant grief, he was renewing us every
day. We never lost hope. We agreed with the Apostle
Paul that somehow all this was for "an eternal weight
of glory" (2 Corinthians 4:17).

I hadn't been home ten minutes when Debbie told
me how people had already begun to reach out to

us with sincere expressions of love and sacrificial acts of kindness.

Over the course of the week we were blessed by our extended family, Cherith's church family, her college friends, our FBC family, the Tres Dias community, our Wednesday night small group, and hundreds and hundreds of others, too many to mention by name.

From all over the world they came with their visits, hugs, phone calls, cards, flowers, meals, texts, emails, Facebook posts, prayers—responses that were beyond belief.

God's love to us was like the ocean waves that keep coming back to the shore. Day after day his mercy continually soothed our grieving hearts. I don't know how people make it through life's tragedies without friends, relatives, or a church family who loves God and who loves you.

The ladies in the neighborhood Bible study that Debbie co-leads with Beverly Dingley kept close watch on our family. I don't recall a day during the first three months when Beverly didn't come by our house or call to see how Debbie was doing.

Bob and Jeanne helped us think through the immediate need to schedule a memorial service. We settled on the day after Mother's Day. Then, Bob, Destiny, and I drove to Macedonia Memorial Park near Canton where we picked out a beautiful burial plot.

It meant so much for Pastor Crawford, and his wife Karen, to come over one evening and pray with our family. We were also pleased to have an encouraging visit from Jason Gerdes, the pastor of Cherith's church.

The celebration of Cherith's life was held on Monday morning, May 12, 2014. Tim Beard, one of FBC's pastors, read from Psalm 139 to give us comfort in knowing that Cherith's days on earth were exactly numbered by God. Like the brook in the Bible, she appeared for a season...and purpose.

The auditorium was filled with over five hundred people. Relatives came from all over. My brother Larry and his family, two of my brother Roger's daughters, Debbie's mom and sisters and their families, and many cousins made it to the ceremony. Cherith's college dorm mates and friends attended and Dave Warren rearranged his schedule and flew in from Nebraska.

The music was unbelievable—the words will forever resonate in our hearts. Robby and the worship band from Revolution Church, where Cherith attended, led four of our favorite songs: *Great is Thy Faithfulness, 10,000 Reasons, Oceans,* and *In Christ Alone.*

Jenna Ellis, the leader of the children's ministry at her church, shared how much the children loved Cherith. Phil and Debbie Gerlicher from First Financial Security told of Cherith's influence at work. Destiny courageously represented the family with powerful words about Cherith's impact on our family.

We heard about the humorous side of Cherith from her college roommate, Tara Stack. She shared how in college the two of them would disguise their voices over the phone and prey on freshman guys, asking if they had any one-armed shirts they could donate to a family whose son had knocked his arm off in a run-in with a wall during a sibling scuffle.

As I scanned the audience, I noticed several of Cherith's coworkers and was reminded of how much she loved them. She prayed for them by name every day.

Jason Gerdes delivered a powerful message from Romans 15:13 on "The God of Hope." He gave a clear presentation of the gospel. At the close he asked people to raise their hands if they were accepting Christ and several gave indication that they were placing their faith in him.

Many people came up to our family afterwards to assure us of their love and prayers. I will never forget the look in their eyes. My friend, Steve Grimes, who serves at the City of Refuge in downtown Atlanta, made his way over to me to announce he had named their new safe home for women the House of Cherith.

We would learn later that people half way around the world were interceding for us at that very moment. Dr. Loritts and Bob Roland happened to be on a trip to Israel with a group from our church and couldn't attend the service. However, while they were in a boat on the Sea of Galilee, they paused to pray for our family.

Art Vander Veen sent us an email to express his love and let us know of his prayers. Here's a portion of what he wrote:

> With all the love and kindness and sensitivity that I can express I remind you

(of Psalm 139) that Cherith did not die a day ahead of time. She went to be with Jesus right on schedule...You can take comfort in the truth that it wasn't just happenstance or chance or some kind of bad luck that ended her life here on this earth. There is a much bigger story being written...a story that someday we will be able to read and understand better than we can today.

Now you know why we have shed tears of sorrow *and* tears of joy. God turned our big burden into a big blessing. Time and time again, all throughout our forty years of marriage, and especially in times of adversity, we have cried out to him and he has always been there to provide. We have learned emphatically that with God, behind every *no* there is always a bigger *yes!*

We have been humbled. Our hearts have been broken. I know I will need daily doses of grace for the rest of my life. Debbie and I are depending on the Holy Spirit, who promised to give us peace and joy in the journey.

And you know what? Every follower of Christ has the same Holy Spirit that's living inside of us. We can all cry out, "Abba! Father!" Each one of us can rely on him for strength to make it through whatever comes our way.

***

Two weeks following Cherith's death I followed through on a commitment I had made six months earlier. BHU had asked me to teach the summer school course *Wisdom Literature* (Psalms, Proverbs, Job).

I remember thinking to myself, "Mike, really? How can you even think about teaching this class when your daughter just died?"

I asked the students to introduce themselves and tell about their family. The first to speak was Tim. He said he had a thirty-two year-old son who had died a year ago that very day. Next, Marie told how her twenty-four year old son, Henry, was killed in a car accident a year ago that same week.

When it came to be my turn I said, "Tim, Marie, we have something in common. My daughter's memorial service was one week ago." I paused for a moment, and then continued, "I think God has something special in mind for our class this summer, don't you?"

A few Sundays later, I taught a two-week series in the Crossroads Class. Richard Henslee, the class leader, had asked me back in January if I would come and teach in June and what I thought my topic would be.

I said, "What about Job?" And so, I spoke on the reasons why we can anchor our hope in God.

Other opportunities came along to bear witness of God's faithfulness. I officiated the wedding for Ariyel and Kari Carver, a young couple that had completed their premarital counseling right before Cherith died.

One of the relatives came up to me moments before the ceremony and asked, "Are you the one who recently lost a daughter?" I answered that I was, and he went on to say that God had given him a verse of Scripture that morning that he believed was intended for me.

He read from Isaiah 57:1: "Good people pass away; the godly often die before their time...No one seems to understand that God is protecting them from the evil to come" (NLT).

Was it possible that in her death God was protecting Cherith?

Surely this tragedy hadn't taken him by surprise. We accept that his timing was perfect. But, did it have a purpose?

CHAPTER 26

Why?

Unless a grain of wheat falls into the earth and dies...

—John 12:24

The folk tale *Chicken Little* is based on the mystery of the acorn that fell from the sky. A plunk on the head was enough to convince Henny Penny that the world was coming to an end. Her sense of despair blocked out the truth. Nonetheless, she sets out on a journey to warn the king.

Along the way she announces the ominous news: "The sky is falling! I'm on my way to warn the king!" Her barnyard friends, Turkey Lurkey, Goosey Loosey, and Foxy Loxy, raise the question, "How do you know the sky is falling?"[23]

Naturally, family and friends had foreboding questions following Cherith's death. "Why? Why did she have to die? Why now?" These clouded questions needed clear answers, based on truth.

Cherith trusted in Christ as her Savior when she was a little girl. I remember the night she sat on my lap and prayed to receive God's gift of eternal life. Based on the truth of Scripture, Debbie and I are confident that Cherith is now with the Lord Jesus in heaven, alive and enjoying eternal life.

When Lazarus died, Jesus made a promise to his sisters, Mary and Martha: "Whoever believes in me, though he die, yet shall he live, and everyone who lives and believes in me shall never die" (John 11:23, 25).

Eternal life is a gift we receive when we place our trust in Christ alone for our salvation (Romans 6:23). When a believer dies, they immediately go to be with Jesus in heaven. On the cross, he told the penitent thief that he would soon join him in Paradise (Luke 23:43).

This is a word Jesus used to describe what heaven was like. It comes from the Persian word *pairidaeza*. It was often used to describe the Persian king Cyrus' royal palace and walled in garden.[24] Here, Jesus is talking about the eternal state, an actual, physical place with God in his heavenly palace that has an enclosed garden—much like the Garden of Eden.

The Apostle Paul said that it is "far better" to be with Christ (Philippians 1:23). He relates that when we are "absent from the body," then we are present with the Lord (2 Corinthians 5:8). We will be clothed with a "heavenly dwelling" (a house not made with hands) until our earthly body is resurrected (2 Corinthians 5:2-4; 1 Corinthians 15:35-49).

On the Mount of Transfiguration, Moses and Elijah were seen in their "glorious splendor" (Luke 9:28-36). When Stephen was being stoned, he looked up to heaven and saw "the glory of God, and Jesus standing at the right hand of God" (Acts 7:55-56).

Dr. Loritts recently completed a three-year preaching series on the Gospel of Matthew. Every Sunday morning he would remind the audience of our purpose in life: "We exist to serve the interests of the King and his Kingdom."

No doubt about it—according to the Bible, our Cherith was born for heaven. She belongs to the King. And, someday we will see her in splendor and beauty! This is truth, a theological understanding.

Yet, even though our faith was strong, our humanity was questioning. We weren't ready to let our daughter go—after all, Cherith was only thirty-three when she died.

In seeking answers to our questions I turned to a meaningful conversation Jesus once had with his disciples. He gave them (and us) an analogy of physical law to understand a spiritual law:

> The hour has come for the Son of Man to be glorified. Truly, truly, I say to you, unless a grain of wheat falls into the earth and dies, it remains alone; but if it dies, then it bears much fruit. (John 12:24-25)

Here, Jesus is illustrating how a seed (grain of wheat) reaches its full development by dying. The sower must allow the seed to die. To hold on to the seed would prevent it from obtaining its best use. The seed was not really alive unless it died.

Jesus is the seed, and his death became true life, releasing an inner life-power and multiplying itself so that many could believe in him and have eternal life. His journey to the cross was necessary—he had to die so that we might live.

When Jesus died at thirty-three, the gospel multiplied. How else would the world be redeemed? Through his death there would be a great harvest. There would be much fruit, many seeds, and deeper truth. The pathway to glory for Christ was through death.

In a similar way, some of those who follow Christ will be called upon to make sacrifices, just as he did. Cherith faithfully followed the Lord and was willing to give up her life and her ambitions for the sake of the Kingdom.

When my dad died at forty-one, his ministry did not end. It continued through his four children and grandchildren. When Jim Elliot died at twenty-nine, his ministry multiplied. God raised up a church among the Aucas. Many people became missionaries who spread the gospel around the globe.

There's a deeper truth. Maybe God had planned all along for Cherith's death to be at a tender age, because he wanted to take her life (seed) and multiply it (bear much fruit) around the world.

We do know this. Within twenty-four hours of Cherith's death her story began to produce spiritual fruit. A girl in Kansas read about Cherith on Facebook from a post written by the mother of one of Cherith's college friends. She responded by saying she wanted to have the assurance of her salvation and the mom prayed with her.

There were several others who placed their faith in Christ during Cherith's memorial service. I have reason to believe that there will be many more who decide to follow Christ—perhaps some after reading this chapter.

Cherith's death produced life-giving fruit. Within seventy-two hours of her death, at least three people got a second chance on life through her organ donations. Imagine getting a phone call and hearing a voice say, "We found a match!" Here's how one family thanked us:

> My family and I would like to offer our condolences on the loss of your loved one. We want you to know how grateful we are for your generous gift. The liver went to a sixty-three-year-old man...and he is grateful for his second chance at life.
>
> We have been married for thirty-nine years and have two married sons. In a few months he will be a grandfather for the first time. Because of your gift he will be around to meet his granddaughter and watch her grow up...You and your loved ones will always be in our prayers.

Could it be that God wanted to use Cherith more in her death than in her life? Was the reason for her death so that many others will come to believe in Christ? Was the reason in part to extend the physical life of others?

My friend, Kelley Johns, gave me a book to read called *When God Weeps* by Joni Earekson Tada and Steve Estes. The authors share several in-depth reasons from God's perspective as to why we go through suffering.

One that connected with me was hearing God say, "I have permitted in your life what I have, so that something eternal and wonderful will be achieved—life, rich, and meaningful on earth, and life in heaven, free of pain and full of joy."[25]

We need to be careful of "Chicken Little" theology—trumping up theories for tragedies. Job's three friends blamed suffering on the sufferer. But, what really caused Job's trials? Were they the result of bad weather, evil people, Satan? No—God. He permits fatal events for his purposes.

Debbie and I have peace in knowing that God is sovereign and that he is achieving what he wants for our lives!

I've found that what Steve Estes said is true: "God permits what he hates to achieve what he loves."[26]

I know death breaks the Father's heart. He weeps for us and with us as we suffer human loss. And, I also know he didn't leave us here on earth to try and figure out why bad things happen to those we love. We turn to his timeless Word and rest in his steadfast love to keep us on track.

As kids, we jokingly quoted John 11:35 as the shortest verse in the Bible. You remember—"Jesus wept." Now that I'm older I'm so thankful that Jesus weeps with us when a loved one dies. I'm comforted by the words of the psalmist who wrote:

> You have kept count of all my tossing and put my tears in your bottle. Are they not in your book? (Psalm 56:8)

***

Because of the great work she provided to their company, Phil and Debbie Gerlicher had honored Cherith by inviting her to be one of the select few who went from the home office each year to "work" on the cruise. After all, it was to honor the highest selling sales associates, but some support staff was needed.

That year's Mediterranean cruise was promoted as the *Dream Destination*. These words could not be more descriptive of where Cherith is now—heaven!

We are so thankful for Laura Manzer, Director of Marketing and Communication with FFS, who was Cherith's dear friend. The two had spent many hours together on the cruise and ports of call. Laura recounted for us all the places they shopped—even details about Cherith's giddy delight over purchasing gifts for her family.

At their company's annual sales meeting, Phil presented the 2014 Leadership Award to Cherith posthumously. Debbie and I can't thank FFS enough for the lasting investment they made in our daughter's life.

***

I was asked to speak at a Tres Dias women's retreat in northeast Georgia. It was only a few months after Cherith's death, but I felt I needed to remain on the team. It was an amazing weekend, as always. Many women's lives were transformed by God's grace.

Saturday night I began praying to the Lord that he would give me a word of encouragement in light of Cherith's death. The next morning, before the Sunday chapel, I went into the meeting room ahead of everyone else and sat on the back row. Rachel Schleier, one of the team members, was a ballerina and she was practicing her routine behind a white screen silhouette to the song *In Christ Alone*. This was one of the songs sung at Cherith's memorial service.

Rachel danced a dance of joy and freedom. The Holy Spirit whispered in my ear. "This is Cherith in heaven! She's with Jesus, having the time of her life, with the love of her life!" My heart felt like it doubled in size. The tears continued to run down my face as Rachel performed it live before all the ladies.

It occurred to me that I wouldn't be able to walk my daughter down the aisle and give her hand in marriage. So, I gave her hand to Jesus, instead.

CHAPTER 27

Our Father

Honey, you've got to come here and see this!

—Debbie

On the morning of September 4, 2014, I woke up with excruciating pain in my lower right side. Bob Roland drove me to the ER at Northside Cherokee Hospital in Canton, all the while thinking it might be a kidney stone.

A nurse wired me up for an EKG. Then, someone carted me off to do a CT scan. When I returned, I was given a large dose of pain medication. It was too much—the sensation was overwhelming. I struggled to breathe.

Realizing I was in a crisis, Bob put his arms around me and whispered in my ear. "It's alright Mike. You're going to be okay. It's almost over." He did that for over *thirty* minutes.

Bob and I had shared a humorous moment in the early years of Fellowship. He volunteered me to help him build a makeshift baptistery out of plywood for the church to use at its initial baptism in the new building. Everyone ran for their lives when the weakened structure exploded while the last person was being immersed. Water flooded everywhere!

However, this moment was serious. In a time of dire uncertainty, I was overcome by God's peace. It literally felt like my heavenly Father was hugging me and assuring me of his presence.

The doctor came in and reported that the CT scan showed I had a kidney stone—but there was more. They found a large tumor on my right kidney. And, my EKG revealed that I had atrial flutter, causing an abnormal heart rhythm. I was experiencing renal and heart failure at the same time.

Larry and Dee Goar and Dr. Loritts arrived at the hospital to pray over me. Bob notified the other church staff and elders to pray. I was prepped for surgery. The stone was successfully removed and my condition stabilized.

An MRI showed clearly that the tumor was malignant. It lit up like a Christmas tree under the x-ray light. Three doctors agreed that the tumor was in a bad location and scheduled me to have a radical nephrectomy in two weeks.

Our friends from Tres Dias, Montell and Kathy Jordan, came over to our house to pray over us. Dr. Herman Alb, Danny and Laura Taylor, and the Guatemala mission team leaders at FBC, also gathered around us to intercede on my behalf. We agreed together and asked God to remove the cancer.

One night I was lying on my pillow, anticipating the upcoming surgery. While Debbie was asleep, I was restless, questioning God about why all these physical challenges were happening.

Was this the discipline of God the Father so that I might "share his holiness" (Hebrews 12:10)? Like Simon Peter, had my "love" for the Lord gone cold (John 21:17)? Was this my walk through "the valley of the shadow of death" (Psalm 23:4)?

I remember wondering why I felt so sad. The truth struck me—it was because I missed my dad. I longed to talk to him and know the answers to all my questions.

That's when my eyes were opened to my heavenly Father. I began to quote the Lord's Prayer, "Our Father..." and then I stopped. I could sense he was entering the room and coming to my bedside. I imagined him pulling down the covers and climbing in bed to lie beside me.

He stroked my hair and hugged me with a warm embrace. I heard him say, "Michael, I love you. You belong to me. Everything will be okay." His message to my soul assured me that I would live and that I needed to be here for Debbie and the family.

Whenever I find myself in a stressful situation, I try to put into practice a method of prayer that I learned from Brennan Manning.[27] While I take in a slow, deep breath, I whisper, "Abba." Then I slowly exhale, saying, "I belong to you." I repeat this several times and he always gives a calming peace.

A few days later, there was a knock at the front door. Bob had called and asked if he and a few others could come over and pray with us. Debbie went upstairs to let him in. But, when she opened the door I heard her say in a loud voice, "Honey, you've got to come here and see this!"

I was in pajamas, but slowly made my way to the foyer to look out the door. To my surprise, as far as my eye could see, my beloved coworkers were getting out of their cars, and like ants, scurrying into our front yard. This precious assembly had driven out to our home to pray with us and bless us.

Four of the pastors, along with my Administrative Assistant, Lisa Montgomery, bounded up the steps and met inside to pray over me. I distinctly felt Tim Beard's hand on my right side and hearing him as he prayed that God would remove the cancer from me.

While they were praying inside, the rest of the staff was circling the outside of our house, holding hands and praying out loud. Then, they sang, *Great is Thy Faithfulness*. Debbie and I were speechless. It was as if we were surrounded by a host of angels and given a significant reminder of the Father's love for us!

On October 8th Dr. Scott Miller performed surgery at Northside Hospital to remove my right kidney. He told my daughter Destiny in post op that he was confident the cancer had not spread.

A week later when I went for the follow up visit, Dr. Miller looked at me bewildered. "I don't know what to say Mr. McCrum. You must have had a lot of people praying for you. The pathology report came back. The tumor we were convinced was cancerous... was benign!"

The day before Thanksgiving I had heart ablation surgery. Lisa and her husband, Pete, stayed in the waiting room and prayed during the eight-hour procedure. Dr. Caesar Cruz set my heart rhythm back to normal and no blood clots were found. This made our family extra thankful that year.

The year 2014 was a difficult one for our family. It was godly friends that kept us going. People like, J. D. Klein, and Anna and Bob Breneman, drove me to follow-up doctor appointments. Dick Roth blessed us with much needed yardwork. It was amazing to see God's love in action—a continual reminder of his faithfulness.

***

I love being on staff at Fellowship Bible Church and serving as Care Ministry Pastor! I'm a shepherd, caring for the sheep. Each day I get out of bed I can hardly wait to get to the church office. You want to know why?

I live for the weekly adventure of teaming with God to rescue marriages and saving families in crises. I especially enjoy premarital counseling and helping couples grow toward intimacy. I may officiate a wedding one day and speak at a funeral the next. I could be at the hospital congratulating parents on their new bundle of joy or praying with a member before going into surgery.

I could be speaking on *Revelation* in a Sunday morning class or teaching *Apocalyptic Literature* to my BHU students on Tuesday nights. I could be speaking at our men's Fellowship Institute (5:30 a.m.) or to our residency church planters. I could be helping organize a major men's event or developing the next support group ministry.

What I enjoy most is discipling men and women and equipping them to serve as high-capacity volunteers in the Care Ministry (2 Timothy 2:2). My passion is to extend myself, my experience, my skills, my education, my calling, into the lives of others who will become inspiring leaders for the sake of the Kingdom.

I pour myself into the lives of others, seeking to encourage and cheer them on, rather than doing everything myself. I connect with the "multiplier versus diminisher" approach that Liz Wiseman introduces in her book *Multipliers*. I'd rather not be the genius, but enable others to become "genius-makers."[28]

We are very blessed to have Larry and Dee Goar and Marilyn Shinn lead *Stephen Ministry*. Bill Dowd has helped train over a hundred FBCers to be Stephen Ministers who can provide one-on-one care to those who are hurting.

Walking Free, led by Tim Carpenter and Tony Eyl, is our very vital ministry to men who struggle with sexual addiction. Alongside them, Cindy Carey, Peggy Yates, Ann McColl, and Heather Creech lead *Journey*, a ministry to the women and wives impacted by men with sexual struggles. These vital ministries would not be possible if not for the encouragement, support, and training by Troy and Melissa Haas with Hope Quest.

GriefShare was developed in the 1960s by David and Nancy Guthrie and its group format is designed for those who have lost a loved one. Steven and Terri Cagle came forward to lead this ministry after I preached a sermon on how to deal with life's tragedies two months following Cherith's death. They, too, had tragically lost a child. *GriefShare* was a tremendous encouragement for Debbie and me during our walk through grief.

Linda Carver, whose husband Don died six years ago, participated in the initial grief pilot group and now, with the assistance of Miriam Brown and Karen Pierce, leads our ministry to widows called *Crown of Beauty.*

Geoff Wiggins serves as Care Minister and leads the Care Ministry Team. He oversees our hospital visitation and sees that appropriate follow-up care is provided. This vital team includes Linda Carver, Tony Erredia, Lynn Woodard, Jo Ann Atkins, Carol Klingler, George and Barbara Deuel, Suzanne Sweatt, and Babs Williams.

Additionally, I serve on the Ordination Board with Tim Beard, Dr. Loritts, and Bob Roland, preparing gifted men for full-time ministry. I also assist Tim with our Church Planting Residency program.

In 2015, Cindy Spitler became my Administrative Assistant. The Care Ministry would not be possible without Cindy's phenomenal, Christ-like servanthood. She ties every ministry together.

I am so fortunate to have the best job on earth. I get to bless others with the Father's love and teach them how to trust God!

CHAPTER 28

There's More

God is calling us to himself...
                        —Paul David Tripp

In the early dawn of May 5, 2016, I was waiting for the seven o'clock alarm to go off. In those reflective moments I prayed a simple prayer, "Father, what do you want me to do today?"

My first thoughts turned to Debbie. It was the two-year anniversary of our daughter's death and I thought the best thing might be to stay home and be with her.

But, at breakfast we agreed that a young couple in our church needed me more. Their three-month-old son, Caleb, had unexpectedly died two days before. I contacted Matt and Sterling and scheduled a pastoral visit for 10:00 a.m.

Before I headed out the door, I decided to call my barber, Blanca Blick, and ask if she had an opening in her schedule. I would either be officiating or assisting in four funeral services over the next ten days and Debbie pointed out my hair was almost to ponytail stage.

"Yes, how does 11:30 a.m. work?" Blanca offered.

"Perfect," I replied. "I'll take it."

As I walked up to the front door to the Norris' home I paused for a quick prayer. "Father, what do I say?" He said, "Tell them you're here to bring them hope."

As I stepped inside, I found myself entering into the depths of the human soul. I listencd intently to the cries of their heart and was deeply moved by their tears of sorrow. I shared with them the stages of grief and how this part of their journey would be a roller coaster of unsettling emotions—shock, denial, isolation, anger, bargaining, guilt, and depression.[29]

I wcpt with them. I prayed over them. I read the promises of hope that had helped Debbie and I make it through our tragedy.

Then the question came—"Will the pain get better?"

It took a few seconds for my heart to catch up with what my head already knew. I thought about our journey and what happened to Cherith. I shared that we endured by trusting in God's sovereignty and depending on him, one day at a time. Eventually, he turned our sorrow into joy.

From there I drove to my 11:30 a.m. hair appointment. As I sat down in the barber chair, Blanca asked, "So, how is your day going?"

It had been sort of a melancholic morning. My heart was still aching for the parents of four

University of Georgia students who were tragically killed in a car accident two weeks before.

I told her I had just come from a visit with a young couple that was grieving the devastating loss of their baby. Then, I reminded her that it was the two-year anniversary of our daughter's sudden death.

I no sooner finished talking about Cherith when the man sitting in the barber chair next to me suddenly slumped forward. Was he having a heart attack? While people watched in disbelief, Blanca dialed 911.

I quickly threw off my apron and rushed over to the man. I took his pulse...*thirty*...that was way too low. I held him in my arms and said, "Sir, look into my eyes. You're gonna be okay! You're gonna make it!"

He tried to focus, but it was obvious—he was slowly fading. Thankfully, within minutes the ambulance arrived and he was rushed to nearby North Fulton Hospital.

When I sat back in my chair Blanca said, "Good thing you were here to help that poor man." Remember, this was the one appointment slot she had available. (I learned later that the man had survived, and after receiving a pace-maker, he was enjoying life!)

I drove to the church office, wondering what could possibly happen next. Another family had just lost their loved one and was requesting that I speak at the funeral service on Saturday. I would assist Shane Freeman with the Norris' memorial service at 1:00 p.m. and leave from there to serve the other family at 3:00 p.m. I took the rest of Thursday afternoon to prepare for both services.

When I arrived home that evening for dinner, Debbie met me at the door and asked, "So, how was your day?"

I smiled and said, "You better sit down. You won't believe what all happened."

***

It seems hardly a week goes by that Debbie and I aren't consoling a grieving family or giving hope to someone in crisis. True to his Word, we have been comforted by God in our affliction and now he uses us to comfort others with the same affliction (2 Corinthians 1:4).

There's hidden treasure buried in that passage of Scripture. God meets us in our pain and sorrow. But then there is "more" he wants to accomplish for his glory!

We have experienced what Paul David Tripp talks about in his book, *Instruments in the Redeemer's Hands*. He writes, "God is calling us to himself in order to change us, so that we can be instruments of the same kind of change in others."[30]

How does this play out? Because Christ's Spirit is embodied in us, we share his dynamic power. Working in and flowing through every believer, it can transform our heart, not only giving us divine energy to face the situations of life, but to help strengthen others in their affliction.

The event that set the course of direction for my life had been my father's "untimely" death. The stories of God's faithfulness that followed, including the events surrounding Cherith's death, confirmed our journey had a purpose: to glorify God by leaving a legacy for the next generation and to inspire weary travelers along the way.

On his way to the cross Jesus pointed out to his disciples that the journey is like a vineyard (John 15:1-12). The Father is the gardener who seeks to grow and produce beautiful fruit. Jesus is the vine, the source of the fruit, and his followers are the branches, or fruit-bearers.

Day by day we can grow and become more like Christ. As we mature in him, he manifests his attitudes and actions in and through us—love, joy, and peace (John 15:9-11; Galatians 5:22-23). The Father constantly changes us because there is more fruit to bear—more opportunity to honor, reward, and glorify him (John 15:8).

Our growth often requires pruning (John 15:2). Even though painful, this allows us to bear even more fruit. Christ's work in us is what Walk to Emmaus (spiritual retreat organization) refers to as "the doctrine of the more." God has more love, more power, more peace, and more joy in store for us so that we can bless more people. Each time we become the face, the hands, and feet of Jesus.

The Holy Spirit equips us with gifts that are needed for the journey (1 Corinthians 12-14; Romans 12:3-8; 1 Peter 4:8-11). There are two ways the word equip (Greek, *katartizó*) was used in the New Testament: (1) to mend a net (Matthew 4:21) and (2) to restore for proper use (Galatians 6:1)[31]. In a spiritual way, Jesus beautifully chooses to mend us and restore us in order to equip others.

Growth is a natural process because we are connected to Jesus, the healthy vine. As branches, we abide in him through prayer (John 15:4). We pray, "Jesus, cut on me, prune me, break me, do whatever you need to do in order for me to be like you and to bear more fruit for you!" His word abides in us and we learn to love him and follow his ways (John 15:7).

Then, our Father desires we open our eyes to recognize those around us who are in desperate need of hope. When prompted by the Spirit, we have the privilege of sharing our growth in grace with the Body of Christ by responding with joyful participation in his missional sufferings.

This is our story and the purpose for which we've been called. God has used each earthly sorrow to produce more fruit in us that yields eternal rewards:

> Beloved, do not be surprised at the fiery trial when it comes upon you to test you, as though something strange were happening to you. But rejoice insofar as you share Christ's sufferings, that you may also rejoice and be glad when his glory is revealed. (1 Peter 4:12-13)

For those on the journey there's more ahead—much more fruit to bear. God is purposefully changing us into the image of his son, so that we will become instruments of change and bring him *more* glory!

CHAPTER 29

Surprise!

Your sorrow will turn into joy...and no one
will take your joy from you.

—John 16:20, 22

I nearly jumped out of my skin! Debbie, our three
children, and our grandkids, along with the help
of my mischievous friend, Bob Roland, planned a
surprise 60th birthday party for me at the church
office.

Bob had done a great job of distracting me at a
nearby doughnut shop. He timed it just right so that
the two of us would arrive a few minutes late to the
staff meeting.

So, when he opened the door to the room,
everyone yelled "Surprise!" I thought I was going
to have a heart attack! After I got over the shock,
my family surrounded me with smiles, kisses, and
hugs. It was an unforgettable moment.

I wonder. When it's our time to step from humanity into eternity, will it be like we're stepping into a surprise birthday party?

There is a dramatic scene in John 16, when Jesus spoke to his disciples and tells of his impending separation. He prepares them for the terror of his trial, his imminent death, and the devastation that stands before him and his followers.

Then, he adds a divine caveat. In this critical moment he tells them about joy:

> You will be sorrowful, but your sorrow will turn into joy...You have sorrow now, but I will see you again and your hearts will rejoice, and no one will take your joy from you. (John 16:20-24)

After Jesus died on the cross and arose from the grave he appeared to the disciples. When they saw his resurrected body, and that he had denied death its finality, their sorrow turned into joy.

In his *Leadership Journal* article on "Joy," Earl Palmer writes, "What they thought might be a permanent loss, producing fear and grief, became (surprise!) a victory."[32]

C.S. Lewis would say, "This is the joy that results from knowing the ending to the story, the ending that is better than anyone expected."[33] It is the "gigantic secret" of God (G.K. Chesterton) that the world could never have expected and it "clears the air so we can see things as they really are."

Apparently, Lewis was fascinated with the biblical word joy and wanted his readers to understand that true joy is profoundly found in the person of Jesus Christ. He describes it as a "species of joy," a shaft of light that comes into a room, pointing to the real source (Jesus) and giving us the sense that everything is okay.

One of the effects of joy is peace. Jesus said, "In *me* you may have peace. In the world you will have tribulation. But take heart; I have overcome the world" (John 16:33).

Debbie and I are learning that sorrow and joy produce a beautiful rhythm. This is the antinomy of Hebrews 12:2, which says, "Who for the joy set before him endured the cross." Joy was not some "dangling carrot" for Jesus. There had to be a sense of joy, even amid the anguish.[34]

We are discovering how to follow our joy (Jesus). This happens when we stay close to him and listen to his Word. That way, when tragedy strikes, we won't get stuck or wander too far off the path he has mapped out for us.

We have an honorable calling from God. Christ left us an example "to follow in his steps" (1 Peter 2:22). Joy gives us the strength we need to walk the journey. "The joy of the Lord is my strength" (Nehemiah 8:10). Jesus invites us to be in a continual attitude of prayer so our joy "might be full" (John 15:1-17).

The Apostle James gives what may seem like an inauspicious challenge: "Count it all joy when you meet trials of various kinds" (James 1:2). We can only do that as we learn to rest in him.

I read about when Zig Zigler's daughter died he said, "I kept thinking my daughter was wondering when her daddy was going to come get her."[35] The Lord spoke in such a distinct way: "She's fine. She's with me. And you're going to be fine, too. I'm all you need. You just keep walking, keep talking, keep praying, keep crying."[36]

***

My favorite Michael Card song is *Joy in the Journey*. He sings about the limitless joy we have from knowing and loving Christ. It provides "a hope for the hopeless and sight for the blind" and "for those who belong to eternity, but who are stranded in time."[37]

In May 2014, Debbie and I were stranded in time. For months, our emotions wouldn't cooperate. Our hearts kept trying to tell us there was no reason to sing. But by Christmas, we were presented some pretty significant gifts which gave us reason to rejoice!

My recovery from two major surgeries was progressing better than expected. Receiving the news that I was cancer-free was a welcome surprise.

We received a newsletter from Palimi-U station where we served in the jungles of Brazil. Dan and Krista Brown had moved there and continued the ministry. He wrote about an incredible incident that just happened in their village.

Unbeknown to us, in the 1960s pioneer missionary Bob Cable had traveled upriver and made contact with the Hokoma people. He shared the gospel with them, but there was no apparent response. For fifty years the missionaries had not seen nor heard from this nomadic tribe—until now.

It turns out that some of the children in that village had listened to Bob and believed in Jesus Christ. Now adults, five of them "happened" to travel down river and land at Palimi-U station. Well, imagine the surprise when these men sang some of the old songs and accurately recounted the Bible stories they had heard. There was great celebration at Palimi-U, as there was when we received the news back here in the States.

Another event came as a complete surprise. A few months earlier I had posted on Facebook about my health situation and asked for prayer. A family I grew up with as a child, happened to come across my post. When they replied to say they were praying, I got a lump in my throat. This was a family I had hurt when I was a young boy.

On December 18th I sent a post to one of the family members. I told how I had been praying for over forty years that one day I would have an opportunity to repent of my actions. I said, "I'm so sorry for what I did and the hurt I caused."

A reply came a few hours later. "Michael, since God in Christ Jesus has forgiven you, I too have forgiven you. Apology accepted."

Then, the crowning event that brought great joy to our family came when our daughter Amber blessed us on December 19th with the early arrival of Ansley Dawn. She chose Dawn for her middle name because it was Cherith's middle name. Her birth made the story of the birth of Christ become even more meaningful that year.

***

In 2 Corinthians 12:10 the Apostle Paul gives a very peculiar response to his "thorn in the flesh." In all of the weaknesses, persecutions, and calamities that God asked him to go through, he responds with joy.

I believe this was because he had been caught up into Paradise and had heard (and perhaps seen) a portion of what heaven is like (v 4). This revelation was a preview of what was to come (vv 2-6). He wasn't allowed to boast about the glory he would share with Jesus in heaven, so he chose to glory in his afflictions on earth. Knowing the end of the story, gave him the strength he needed to thrive, not just survive.

Debbie and I look forward to the day when we will join with loved ones in heaven to surround the throne of God and worship the Holy One (Revelation 4). Until then, we continue the sometimes perilous journey God asked us to walk, knowing full well, the end of the story is far better than we could have ever expected.

In heaven, overcomers will sing a new song. Until then, we sing songs of faith to lighten the load on earth. Stuart Hamblen's hymn *Until Then* reminds us of the surpassing joy we can have on our road to see the King:

> My heart will sing when I pause to remember
> A heartache here is but a stepping stone
> Along a trail that's winding always upward,
> This troubled world is not my final home.
>
> But until then my heart will go on singing,
> Until then with joy I'll carry on—
> Until the day my eyes behold the city,
> Until the day God calls me home.[38]

During a particularly difficult time in our journey, when I felt stranded, I asked Bob Roland, "How long will it take?" Remember his response? "Until you can trust God through it and thank him for it."

Along the way, Debbie and I have learned to trust in God's faithfulness. We have thankful hearts. We have joy in knowing all this was to prepare us for what lies ahead. When we get to heaven, we'll look back at our lives on planet earth and hopefully see how we discovered joy in our journey, and say, "It was worth it all!"

A great surprise awaits all of us when we come into the presence of the King. And, nothing in this world can block the truth of what lies ahead: "You make known to me the path of life; in your presence there is fullness of joy; at your right hand are pleasures forevermore" (Psalm 16:11). Joy is the surprise of heaven that sustains us here on earth!

***

I recently attended the AACC (American Association of Christian Counselors) convention that was held in Nashville, Tennessee. The crowd of seven thousand was mesmerized as Joni Eareckson Tada graciously made her way to the podium in her motorized wheelchair. Forty-eight years before she broke her neck in a diving accident that left her a quadriplegic for life.

In her stirring speech she recalled how difficult it was to live those first few years on her back in the hospital. She asked the audience, "Do you want to know how I made it?" I leaned forward and listened carefully.

Joni disclosed that every week a friend would come by and read the Scriptures to her. At first, she endured it because she enjoyed the company. When he left she would listen to Beatles music to try and take away her sadness.

But, at night, like King David in Psalm 18, she would cry out to God and wrestle with why he had allowed this tragedy to happen. It was through hearing God's Word, week after week, over and over, that she put her trust in Christ and accepted his will for her life.

For Joni, and for us, no more practical words were ever written than what the psalmist said in Psalm 119:67: "It was good for me to be afflicted so that I might learn your ways."

Early on, when Debbie and I realized Cherith was fighting for her life, we looked for a reason to hold out hope. The truth that kept us going then is the truth that keeps us going now—since God is always faithful, we can always trust his ways...no matter what!

What's your story?

Know this—whatever adventure God has written for you, there is joy in the journey, because of the surprise at the end!

AFTER WORDS

Like Henny Penny, we are on a journey to see the King. The road of life is full of adventure and there are fearful encounters along the way—brief moments when the sky *is* falling and your world *is* coming to an end.

Debbie and I have experienced the falling sky. We know what it's like to lose a family member to death, to lose your house (tornado), your job, and everything you've owned (Brazil). We've hurt people, and we've been hurt by people. Dear friends have abandoned us; and dear friends have rescued us. And, some of our toughest, but most meaningful moments have come with our children.

Through it all, we've lived a life of purpose by learning to trust God with whatever happens. He has faithfully provided for us time and again. We are thankful for all the good and the (seemingly) bad. In the end, we have so much to rejoice over!

The journey for Debbie and me is not finished. We know there's more to come—the legacy ahead is grand, a reason for which to live and to die. We know God created our marriage in eternity past, to multiply in eternity present, in order to bring glory to him in eternity future.

Looking *backward*, we had to make the journey and experience God's faithfulness in order to tell others with certainty that they can come to know the same God we know. When we see and fully grasp all that he has done, our hearts are filled with great joy! God had so much in mind, more than we could ever have imagined—so many lives to be changed in our lifetime, and more after we're gone...all for him.

Looking *forward*, we especially want our children and their children to continue the story of God's faithfulness and to pass it down to the next generation. In her eBook, *How to Craft a Family Purpose Statement*, Erica Layne provides practical help in developing the "why" of your life.[39]

The "why" in our lives starts with Destiny. She and her husband Jeff Howe, live in Canton, with their four children: Will, Madelyn, Abigail, and Aiden. Next are Amber and Mitchell Myers, who have settled on a twenty-acre farm near Calhoun, with their two children: Lily and Ansley. Then, there's Robby. He is engaged to Susan Hickey and they plan to marry in October, 2016.

DEBBIE: *It had been a long-time dream of mine to have our children live close enough to us after they married and became parents. We wanted to be able to help them through those difficult first years of parenting. I look forward to the opportunities to continue building into the lives of our children, and especially our grandchildren.*

When both parents are at work, I have been blessed to be able to provide childcare for the grandchildren (they call it Grammy's School). It has never been more than a few days per week and allows me to keep my sewing business alive.

We play, watch Veggie Tales, and do lots of crafts together. During the Christmas season the fun times overflow. When you supervise children for an entire day, there are all sorts of opportunities to sing, learn Bible verses, and just have fun.

I will continue to tell our grandkids how we have experienced God's faithfulness and why they should trust in him. We are sure there are more chapters God has for us to live out with our family on earth, but there are many more families in the Body of Christ we can impact with our wisdom and life experience to help them complete their journey.

Looking *upward*, we anticipate a grand family reunion in heaven that's literally out of this world. Cherith was our great party planner and gift giver on earth. She's waiting for the moment when she can shout—"SURPRISE!"

GREAT IS THY FAITHFULNESS

"Great is Thy faithfulness," O God my Father,
There is no shadow of turning with Thee;
Thou changest not, Thy compassions, they fail not
As Thou hast been Thou forever wilt be.

"Great is Thy faithfulness!" "Great
is Thy faithfulness!"
Morning by morning new mercies I see;
All I have needed Thy hand hath provided—
"Great is Thy Faithfulness," Lord, unto me!

Summer and winter, and springtime and harvest,
Sun, moon and stars in their courses above,
Join with all nature in manifold witness
To Thy great faithfulness, mercy and love.

Pardon for sin and a peace that endureth,
Thine own dear presence to cheer and to guide;
Strength for today and bright hope for tomorrow,
Blessings all mine, with ten thousand beside![40]

May the God of hope fill you
with all joy and peace in believing,
so that by the power of the Holy Spirit
you may abound in hope.

Romans 15:13

DEVELOPING A
FAMILY PURPOSE

Questions to Set the Course of Direction

1. Why does our marriage exist?

2. How can we see us glorifying God together?

3. What Scripture(s) will guide us?

4. How will our purpose affect our children and grandchildren?

5. Besides God, who can help us in the journey?

6. What short-term and long-range goals will keep us on track?

7. What will sustain us on the road?

ACKNOWLEDGEMENTS

Thanks to John "Doc" Parrish, Brian Dodd, Miriam Dolson, Sheri Kennedy, and Dr. Loritts for encouraging us to write this book. Thanks "Doc," for editing the manuscript.

Thanks to Rebecca Miller for designing the book cover. Thanks to Russ Ott for helping with the interior layout. Thanks to Bruce Schneider for the author photo.

Thanks to Bob Roland and Tom Grady for showing us the Father.

Thanks to the ladies in Debbie's neighborhood Bible study and our Wednesday night small group who walked the journey with us during our most difficult hours.

Thanks to Crossroads and Trailblazers, and our spiritual retreat communities, who prayed for us throughout the writing process.

Thanks to the families, staff, and elders of FBC, those mentioned in the book and those not mentioned. It is a joy to serve the King with you!

NOTES

1   Crawford Loritts, *For a Time We Cannot See* (Chicago: Moody Press, 2005), 93-95.

2   Rob Reiner, *The Princess Bride* (1987), www.princessbride.8m.com/script.htm, (accessed December 29, 2015).

3   Reiner, *The Princess Bride*, Scene 12.

4   John Eldredge, *Epic: The Story God is Telling and the Role that is Yours to Play* (Nashville: Nelson Books, 2004), 1-2.

5   Eldredge, *Epic*, 1-2.

6   This account was written by Pat Warren for our grandparent's 50th wedding anniversary.

7   Charles T. Studd, *Wikipedia*, https://en.wikipedia.org/wiki/Charles_Studd (accessed December 29, 2015)

8   Frederick Buechner, "Adolescence and the Stewardship of Pain," *The Clown in the Belfry* (New York: Harper Collins Publishers, Inc., 1992), 4-5.

9   Gene Edwards, *A Tale of Three Kings* (Carol Stream: Tyndale House Publishers, Inc., 1980, 1992), 15-18.

10 Quote from a sermon by Dr. Crawford Loritts, *Why are We Here?* (Roswell, Georgia: Fellowship Bible Church, April 10, 2016).

11 Elisabeth Elliot, *Shadow of the Almighty* (New York: Harper & Row, Publishers, 1958), 54.

12 Cornell Capa and Major Malcom Nurnberg, "Martyrdom in Ecuador," *Life*, Volume 40, Number 5 (Chicago: Time, Inc., January 30, 1956), 10-19.

13 Quote from Dr. Greg Miller at *The Fight of Your Life* Men's Conference (Roswell, Georgia: Fellowship Bible Church, January 30, 2016).

14 Joni Eareckson Tada and Steven Estes, *When God Weeps* (Grand Rapids: Zondervan Publishing House, 1997), 215.

15 Quote from a sermon by Brennan Manning, *Come Now, My Love* (Maple Grove, Minnesota: Church of the Open Door, October 2, 1995).

16 Kenneth L. Swetland, *Facing Messy Stuff in the Church* (Grand Rapids: Kregel, 2005), 98.

17 Andrew Purves, *The Crucifixion of Ministry* (Downers Grove: InterVarsity Press, 2007), 10.

18 Reiner, *The Princess Bride*, Scene 15.

19 Reiner, *The Princess Bride*, Scene 15.

20 www.unshackled.org (accessed July 12, 2016).

21 Jacque Wilson and Matt Smith, "Two Inches of Chaos: What Atlanta's Leaders Were Doing While the Snow Fell," www.cnn.com, Posted February 1, 2014 (accessed December 31, 2015).

22 Phillip Yancey, *What Good is God?* (New York: Faith Words, 2010), 85.

23 Henny Penny, *Wikipedia*, https://en.wikipedia.org/wiki/Henny_Penny (accessed December 29, 2015).

24 Randy Alcorn, *Heaven* (Carol Stream, IL: Tyndale House Publishers, Inc. 2004), 55.

25 Tada and Estes, *When God Weeps*, 215.

26 Tada and Estes, *When God Weeps*, 84.

27 Quote from a sermon by Brennan Manning, *Abba, I Belong to You* (Maple Grove, Minnesota: Church of the Open Door, October 3, 1995).

28 Liz Wiseman, *Multipliers* (New York: HarperCollins Publishers, 2010), 10.

29 Elisabeth Kübler Ross, *On Death and Dying* (New York: Scribner, 1969), 51.

30 Paul David Tripp, *Instruments in the Redeemer's Hands* (Phillipsburg, NJ: P&R Publishing, 2002), xi.

31 John Walvoord and Roy B. Zuck, Editors, *The Bible Knowledge Commentary*, "New Testament Edition" (Wheaton, IL: 1983), 635.

32 Earl Palmer, "Joy: Spiritual Health Made Visible," *Leadership Journal* (Carol Stream: Christianity Today, Fall 1998), 35-37.

33 Palmer, "Joy," 36.

34 Ben Patterson and Zig Zigler, "More Oxygen to the Flame," *Leadership Journal* (Carol Stream: Christianity Today, Fall 1998), 22-27.

35 Patterson and Zigler, "Oxygen," 23.

36 Patterson and Zigler, "Oxygen," 23.

37 Michael Card, "Joy in the Journey," *Joy in the Journey* (Brentwoood, TN: Sparrow, 1994).

38 Stuart Hamblen, *Until Then* (Nashville: Paragon Associates, Inc. 1976), 133.

39 Erica Layne, *How to Craft a Family Purpose Statement*, www.letwhylead.com, Posted November 9, 2015 (accessed December 29, 2015).

40 Thomas O. Chisholm and William M. Runyan, *Great is Thy Faithfulness* (Nashville: Paragon Associates, Inc., 1976) 98.

Printed in the United States
By Bookmasters